ISBN: 9781314879124

Published by:
HardPress Publishing
8345 NW 66TH ST #2561
MIAMI FL 33166-2626

Email: info@hardpress.net
Web: http://www.hardpress.net

I wrote this in
Prison

[signature]

EXO-PSYCHOLOGY

⟶ IT lack
the sense of humor that
marijuana could have

BOOKS AND MONOGRAPHS BY THE AUTHOR

The Dimensions of Intelligence (M.S. thesis, W.S.U., 1946)
The Social Dimensions of Personality (Ph.D. thesis, U.C., 1950)
The Interpersonal Diagnosis of Personality (1957)
Multilevel Assessment of Personality (1957)
The Existential Transaction (1960)
The Psychedelic Experience (with Metzner and Alpert, 1964)
The Psychedelic Reader (ed. with Weil, 1965)
Psychedelic Prayers from the Tao Te Ching (1967)
High Priest (1968)
Politics of Ecstasy (1968)
Jail Notes (1971)
Principles and Practice of Hedonic Psychology (1972)
Confessions of a Hope Fiend (1973)
Neurologic (with Joanna Leary, 1973)
Starseed: A Psy-Phy Comet Tale (1973)
The Curse of the Oval Room (1974)
Terra II (with Joanna Leary and L. W. Benner, 1974)
What Does WoMan Want? (1976)
The Periodic Table of Evolution (1977)
Exo-Psychology (1977)
The Eight Calibre Brain (1977)
The Game of Life (1977)
Neuropolitics (1977)
The Sex Goddess and the Harvard Professor (1977)

EXO-PSYCHOLOGY

A MANUAL ON THE USE OF THE HUMAN NERVOUS SYSTEM ACCORDING TO THE INSTRUCTIONS OF THE MANUFACTURERS

TIMOTHY LEARY

A STARSEED/PEACE PRESS PUBLICATION • 1977 • LOS ANGELES, CALIFORNIA

Published Jointly in the United States by
Starseed/Peace Press Inc.
P.O. Box 188
Culver City, California 90230

Manufactured in the United States
Printed by Peace Press Inc.

Library of Congress Cataloging in Publication Data
Catalog Card No.: 76-56056
Leary, Timothy
Exo-Psychology
A Manual on the Use of the Nervous System
According to the Instructions of the Manufacturers
Los Angeles, California
7611   761214
ISBN   0-915238-16-0

Coordinated by Jay Levey

Designed and Illustrated by Cynthia Marsh for Starseed

Typeset by
Caravan Composing & Design
Los Angeles, California

Layout by Linda Norlen

Cover Photograph by Norman Seeff

0 9 8 7 6 5 4 3

"This is not going to be a volume of memoirs about my own life. Therefore I am not going to recount the truly amusing details of my arrest, which was like no other. That night the SMERSH officers gave up their last hope of being able to make out where we were on the map—they had never been able to read maps anyway. So they politely handed the map to me and asked me to tell the driver how to proceed to Central Intelligence at army headquarters. I, therefore, led them and myself to that prison, and in gratitude they immediately put me not in an ordinary cell but in a punishment cell."

Aleksandr L. Solzhenitsyn

"We've got the greatest system in the world; we've just got to find a way to make it work."

Nelson Rockefeller

The purpose of "Life" is

S. M. I^2. L. E.

Space Migration

Intelligence Increase

Life Extension

Since
No one can allow the game
To become bigger than
Hir concept of the Game
            (what is not imprinted
            is not real to the
            primate brain)
Therefore
Let us define the game
as large
    fast
    intense
    precise
as possible . . . .
Unlimited Space
Unlimited Time
and
Unlimited Intelligence to enjoy same.
S.M.I^2. L.E.

This book is dedicated to

evolutionary agents,

on this planet & elsewhere.

PREFACE

Life on the Planet Earth, through the instrumentality of the human nervous system, has begun to migrate from the Womb Planet, to establish colonies in space, from whence it can more accessibly contact and communicate with Life in the Galaxy.

Rocket-ships have attained the escape velocity necessary to ascend beyond the gravitational pull of the womb-planet.

Radio-telescope "dishes" now look out to the stars, ready to receive electromagnetic messages from intelligent neighbors.

Electronic signals are now transmitting through interstellar space the message of human readiness to ex-change and com-unicate.

In our minds, in our neurons, in our cells, we know that we, who are about to leave this small satellite of a peripheral star, are neither alone nor unique.

Within the life-time of many who read these lines, it will happen: our pioneer families will leave the solar system; interstellar messages will be received; contact will be made. The galactic discussion will begin.

It is about time to prepare for life in space.

It is about time to develop a philosophy, a psychology, the language, the confident wisdom to enable us to listen, understand, and respond intelligently to our interstellar neighbors.

The most important and least boring challenge facing humanity is to prepare ourselves neurologically to meet the Einsteinian "relatives" with whom we share the galaxy. The highest priorities—intellectual, social, economic—should be assigned to extra-terrestrial communication and migration.

Some among us will protest that human intelligence and human resources should be used to solve the agonizing terrestrial problems of unequal distribution.

These larval protests, however sincere, are historically wrong and genetically futile.

The cause of the suffering and scarcity which now threatens humanity is not material. It is neuro—political. Does not the current malaise of the affluent nations` demonstrate clearly that material rewards are somehow not enough?

The crisis which the human race now faces has been called spiritual, psychological, philosophic. It is best described as navigational. Humanity has lost the map, the compass, the guide-book; misplaced the genetic code.

There is only one way from down. Up!

Men and women who know from whence they come and where they are going, who share a vision beyond the local-mundane, will learn quickly, work effectively, grow naturally, socialize lovingly, and evolve gracefully. This is because of the genetic Law of Least Effort. It is probably true that both a species and an individual coasts along on serene stupidity until faced with an evolutionary challenge; at which point both the species and the individual become very smarter very faster.

S. M. I^2. L. E.   S. M. I^2. L. E.   S. M. I^2. L. E.   S. M. I^2. L. E.   S. M. I^2. L. E.

World War II provides an interesting example of this genetic acceleration. The basic principles of atomic structure, rocket propulsion, psychedelic neuro-acceleration and radar had been well known for decades. But under the benign pressure of the Technological Imperative, the American and German scientific communities got smart. Fast.

When humanity begins to work for extraterrestrial migration, the competition for material acquisition will gradually diminish because unlimited space, unlimited energy, unlimited resource await in the extra-terrestrial solar system.

Migration is nature's classic solution to the problem of over-population, scarcity, and competition.

The development of Exo-psychologies, scientific philosophies of extraterrestrial neurogenetics is the ticket for creating global, interspecies collaboration.

This book, a simple-minded attempt to provide a galactic perspective of biological evolution on and from this planet, presents hundreds of neogenetic ideas for which the human species is now ready. The transmission is presented in larval muscular-symbol-units (laryngeal-manual) although the topics discussed are post-larval, electro-magnetic and quantum-mechanical. The reader should expect, therefore, that hir conditioned symbol-system is going to be jolted with unexpected and novel symbol combinations. This is exactly the situation that will exist when we begin living in space colonies and when Higher Intelligence begins to communicate with a species of Domesticated Primates like the human race.

A human from the twentieth century would find it a most difficult and delicate task to explain "now" to an average fellow from the eighteenth century. The sophisticated reader can avoid being irritated by some of the metaphors in this book if cultural time-lag is kept in mind.

Some good-will and open-ness towards the future is necessary in interspecies dialogues of this sort.

The importance of this extra-planetary guidebook is that it exists. Here is the first attempt to prepare humanity for the outward journey, for extra-terrestrial union, for extraterrestrial migration.

Other and more sophisticated Exo-psychologies will follow. Is there any more interesting or vital thing to do than to create the future?

This first attempt is deliberately eclectic and translational—linking the religious-occult to the scientific; the mundane to the futique; the legends of the past to the data of the present.

We have defined eight periods and twenty-four stages of neurological evolution as a didactic device to anticipate, to specify, to order, to personalize, to familiarize the immense post-symbolic, meta-personal, post-Newtonian energy-fields which are to be imprinted.

The illustrative metaphors are not important. What is crucial to humanity's graceful mutation is the understanding and personal application of Einsteinian, neuro-genetic, astro-physical perspectives of who we are and to whom we are going.

SPACE MIGRATION   INTELLIGENCE INCREASE   LIFE EXTENSION

TABLE OF CONTENTS

PART I

THE EVOLUTION, STRUCTURE AND FUNCTION OF THE NERVOUS SYSTEM

PART II

THE PERIODIC TABLE OF ENERGY DEFINES TWENTY-FOUR STAGES
OF NEUROLOGICAL EVOLUTION:
TWELVE TERRESTRIAL AND TWELVE EXTRATERRESTRIAL

Period (Circuit of Nervous System)	Stage of Nervous System
1. The Vegetative-invertebrate Circuit (Viscerotonic)	1. Bio-survival Receptivity 2. Bio-survival Intelligence 3. Bio-survival Fusion-synergy
2. The Emotion-locomotion Circuit (Musculotonic)	4. Neuro-muscular Receptivity 5. Neuro-muscular Intelligence 6. Neuro-muscular Fusion-synergy
3. The Laryngeal-manual Symbolic Circuit (Cerebrotonic)	7. Laryngeal-manual (L.M.) Symbolic Receptivity 8. Laryngeal-manual (L.M.) Symbolic Intelligence 9. Laryngeal-manual (L.M.) Symbolic Fusion-synergy
4. The Socio-sexual Domestication Circuit (Generotonic)	10. Socio-sexual Receptivity 11. Socio-sexual Domesticity 12. Socio-sexual Collectivity
5. The Neurosomatic Circuit (Body Consciousness)	13. Neurosomatic Receptivity 14. Neurosomatic Intelligence 15. Neurosomatic Fusion-synergy
6. The Neuro-electric Circuit (Brain Control)	16. Neuro-electric Receptivity 17. Neuro-electric Intelligence 18. Neuro-electric Fusion-synergy
7. The Neurogenetic Circuit (DNA Consciousness)	19. Neurogenetic Receptivity 20. Neurogenetic Intelligence 21. Neurogenetic Fusion-synergy
8. The Neuro-atomic Metaphysiological Circuit	22. Neuro-atomic Receptivity 23. Neuro-atomic Intelligence 24. Neuro-atomic Fusion-synergy

(handwritten in margin) VTANCY ANLY HLIDHIOD (E-DULES).

PART I

THE EVOLUTION, STRUCTURE AND FUNCTION OF THE NERVOUS SYSTEM

EXO-PSYCHOLOGY

The Principles of Interstellar Neurogenetics
Describing the Evolution of the Four larval-terrestrial
and the Four Post-terrestrial Phases of Contelligence;

TOO SPACY

1. Exo-psychology Is the Science Which Studies the Evolution of the Nervous System in its Larval and Post-terrestrial Phases

---

At the same time that psychology was becoming a pop-cult surrogate-religion, the chemical, physical, and biological sciences were quietly producing theories and replicable facts which have profound implications for the understanding of human nature.

Primitive, pre-Einsteinian psychology (1850-1975), while claiming to measure thinking, consciousness and behavior, for the most part studied the adjustment-maladjustment of human beings to social rituals and culturally defined symbol systems. Appearing at a time when orthodox theology was losing its meaning for the growing class of semi-educated, psychology provided a comforting rationale for domestication, a soothing pseudo-scientific language for supporting the values of the middle class.

Primitive psychology, in spite of its enormous, state-supported bureaucracy and its priesthood mystique, has produced no verifiable theory for explaining human behavior nor any methods for solving the classic problems of human society—crime, conflict, alienation, prejudice, stupidity, boredom, aggression, unhappiness, and philosophic ignorance about the meaning of life.

At the same time that psychology was becoming a pop-cult surrogate-religion, the chemical, physical, and biological sciences were quietly producing theories and replicable facts which have profound implications for the understanding of human nature.

Neurology locates the source of consciousness, memory, learning, and behavior in the nervous system—a thirty billion cell bio-computer for which the body is transportational robot.   100

Clearly if we wish to understand and improve our mental, emotional and behavioral functions, the locus of investigation is the nervous system. The person who can dial and tune the receptive, integrative, transmitting circuits of the nervous system is not just more intelligent, but can be said to operate at a higher and more complex level of evolution.

Pre-scientific humans maintain a rigid taboo about discussing or tampering with their nervous systems—a phobia which is based on a primitive fear of the unknown and superstitious reluctance to learn how to know. It is now evident that the nervous system is an incredibly powerful instrument for conscious evolution which can be understood and employed for genetic tasks.

Ethology, which studies animal behavior in the natural and experimental setting, has demonstrated the robot-instinctual nature of neural discrimination and the role of imprinting in determining when, and towards what, animal behavior is initiated. Psychologists have failed to apply the findings of ethology to the human situation. The fact that human emotional, mental, sexual and ethical behavior is based on accidental imprinting of the nervous system during "critical" or "sensitive" periods of development is apparently too devastating to pretensions of free-will and conscious choice.

Neurochemistry has recently discovered that neurotransmitter chemicals which facilitate/inhibit nerve impulses and synaptic connections determine consciousness, emotion, memory, learning and behavior.

We need not be surprised at "man's" flattering, self-appraisal. Since the "island realities" which we inhabit are defined by genetic template and imprint we can only evaluate ourselves in terms of the symbols which our nervous systems have ~~created.~~

various   *alteration*   *imprinted*

Psychopharmacology at the same time has discovered botanical and synthetic psycho-active agents which facilitate/inhibit states of consciousness and accelerate or dampen mental function.

These Einsteinian discoveries have predictably traumatized those psychologists who are committed both professionally and theologically to static, Newtonian, concepts of human personality.

These four sciences provide an impressive convergence of evidence suggesting that the brain is a bio-chemical-electric computer in which each nerve impulse acts as an information "quanta" or "bit"; that the nervous system is structurally wired into genetically pre-programmed circuits designed to automatically select and relay certain perceptual cues and to discharge rote reactions; that imprinting **of models accidentally present in the environment at critical periods determines the tunnel realities in which** humans live.

We are led to conclude that the human being, at this stage of evolution, is a biological robot (biot) automatically responding to genetic template and childhood imprinting.

The unflattering portrait of **homo sapiens** suggested by the evidence from these four "new" sciences—neurology, ethology, neurochemistry, and psychopharmacology—is, of course, quite unacceptable to psychologists and religious leaders who enunciate theories about "man's" separate, superior and "chosen" status among life forms.

We need not be surprised at "man's" flattering, self-appraisal. Since the "island realities" which we inhabit are defined by genetic template and imprint we can only evaluate ourselves in terms of the symbols which our nervous systems have ~~created~~

If we can imagine an anthropological report about **homo sapiens** written by extra-terrestrial scientists from a more advanced civilization, we can assume that humanity's inability to solve its psychological, social and ecological problems or to provide answers to basic cosmological questions (e.g. why are we here and where are we going?) would lead to the conclusion that **homo sapiens is a species capable of very** limited robot-reactivity and that intelligent Life has not yet evolved on this planet.

Such an extra-terrestrial survey could also report the emergence of a rudimentary intelligence, as evidenced by the Einsteinian perspectives of the four sciences just discussed and by the explosive implications of four other sciences which have significance for human destiny in the future:

~~astronautics~~   *BODY CONSCIOUSNESS*   *Psychedelics*
~~astro-physics~~   *CYBERNETIC*
genetics
~~nuclear physics~~   *NANOTECH*

There can be no question that humanity has begun its migration to interplanetary and eventual interstellar existence. The effects of this transition on the nervous system and the DNA code will be profound. Just as amphibian and land-dwelling organisms mutated rapidly, developing the neural and physiological equipment for the new environment—so will space-travelling humans mutate rapidly.

BODY AS VEHICLE

Re de(ic) Astronautics: The significance of extra-terrestrial flight has not yet been fully understood. The Apollo missions were more than technological triumphs or nationalistic achievements. Genetically and neurologically the beginning of a species mutation has occurred—equal in importance to the first amphibian movement from water-to-land early in biological history.

There can be no question that humanity has begun its migration to interplanetary and eventual interstellar existence. The effects of this transition on the nervous system and the DNA code will be profound. Just as amphibian and land-dwelling organisms mutated rapidly, developing the neural and physiological equipment for the new environment—so will space-travelling humans mutate rapidly.

Exposure to zero-gravity and to extra-terrestrial radiation are two of many physical stimuli which will trigger-off the genetic and neurological changes necessary to adapt to interstellar life.

The psychological effects will be dramatic. Space migration requires accelerated, relativistic, multi-dimensional flexibility of which the nervous system is capable. It is inevitable that extra-planetary humans will be as advanced beyond current earth-dwellers as "man" is beyond the cave-dwelling ancestors. The beginnings of this process of exo-psychological adaptation can be noted in several lunar astronauts and E.V.A. veterans who returned claiming cosmic insights (Mitchell), philosophic revelations (Schweikart), and rebirth symptoms (Aldrin).

Astro-physics has also produced facts which stretch the limits of psychological vision. We learn to our delight that we are not alone—that perhaps as many as half of the 100 billion stars in our local galaxy are older than our sun, making it highly probable that more advanced forms of intelligent life are around the neighborhood. Humans have so far been neurologically incapable of conceiving of Higher Intelligence. Even science fiction writers, with very few exceptions (Stapledon, Asimov, Clarke), have been unable to specify the manifestations of superior species, except as technological extrapolations and bizarre extremes of current human culture.

Whatever the mind can conceive it tends to create. As soon as humans accept and neurologically imprint the notion of higher levels of intelligence and of circuits of the nervous system as yet unactivated—a new philosophy of evolution will emerge. It is natural to call this extra-planetary perspective of human evolution Exo-psychology— human nature seen in the context of an evolving nervous system, from the vantage point of older species which now exist in our extra-terrestrial future.

Genetics has revealed that DNA blueprints which reside in the nucleus of every living cell are remarkably similar from species to species. Astronomers and exo-biolo-

The DNA code contains the blueprint of the past and the future. The caterpillar DNA contains the design for construction and operation of the butterfly body.

gists have discovered the molecules which are basic to life in outer space and in other star systems. The DNA code can now be seen as a temporal blueprint unfolding sequentially like a tape-spool, transmitting preprogrammed construction plans. In the individual this code unfolds through predetermined stages from infancy, through childhood, adolescence, maturity, menopause, aging and death. A fixed time schedule similarly unfolds in the evolution of species.

The DNA code contains the blueprint of the past and the future. The caterpillar DNA contains the design for construction and operation of the butterfly body.

It has long been known that individual ontology recapitulates species phylogeny—that the human embryo, for example, repeats the evolutionary cycle; grows gills, is covered with hair, etc. The psycho-neural time-perspective implications of this fact have never been seriously studied.*

Geneticists are just now discovering "unused" sections of the DNA, masked by histones and activated by nonhistone proteins, which are thought to contain the blueprint of the future. Evolution is not a blind accidental, improvising process. The DNA code is a prospective blueprint which can be deciphered.

Just as an engineer could study the flow-charts of an auto-assembly plant and see how a car is put together in a sequence of future operations—so can the histone-masked sections of the DNA code be studied to determine the sequence of future evolution. The instruments for deciphering the DNA message are neurological and neurochemical. The science which studies the two-way communication between DNA-RNA and the nervous system is called **Neurogenetics.**

Astronomy and astronautics persuade us that interstellar travel lies ahead in humanity's future. Extra-terrestrial existence will involve an advanced, mutated nervous system and inevitable contact with superior intelligence.** This new scientific understanding of human destiny might be called **Interstellar Neurogenetics.**

Neurogenetics is a new science (with a respectable journal and membership dues)

---

*The theory of serial imprinting suggests that psychology recapitulates phylogeny. That the individual nervous system repeats the evolutionary sequence. That the baby imprints an invertebrate reality, the crawling child a mammalian reality, the pre-school child a paleolithic reality, the adolescent a domesticated-civilized reality.

**Some astronomers now state that Superior Intelligence does not exist in the universe because "they" have not contacted us or responded to our radio signals. Such conclusions illustrate the negative bias of conventional science. There is, of course, no scientific basis for claiming or denying the existence of Higher Intelligence. Time-dilation factors complicate the matter; if a space ship were hurtling towards us at close to light-speed, millions of years would elapse on earth for every year in flight. There is no basis for dogmatic statement.

Just as the DNA code, located in the nucleus of the cell, is the genetic brain which, via RNA, designs and manufactures bodies and nervous systems, so can we conceive of the nucleus of the atom as the elemental "brain" which designs and constructs atoms and molecules.

which studies the psychology—i.e. the consciousness and behavior—of DNA-RNA. Neurogenetics may be called a branch of exo-psychology if we assume that DNA contelligence is not restricted to planet earth, but, indeed, was probably originated by and designed to return to extra-terrestrial intelligence.

It is becoming clear that the nucleus of the atom is a complex organization of powerful forces which operate according to relationship-laws (excitement, charm, spin parity, resonance). Just as the DNA code, located in the nucleus of the cell, is the genetic brain which, via RNA, designs and manufactures bodies and nervous systems, so can we conceive of the nucleus of the atom as the elemental "brain" which designs and constructs atoms and molecules according to quantum logic.

Nuclear Physics: It is now believed that all matter and energy in the universe operates in a "general field" which can be understood in terms of the relativistic interaction among the four basic forces that exist in nature:

> gravitational
> electro-magnetic
> **Strong force (subatomic)**
> weak force (radiational).

Primitive psychology was based, at best, on Newtonian "laws" and, for the most part, was geocentric (closet Ptolemaist). Even the most poetic Freudians, Behaviorists and transactional analysts have not allowed their theories of human behavior to be influenced by the Einsteinian revolution which has so dramatically changed our understanding of the structure of the universe.

Neurophysics is the science which is just beginning to study the "psychology"—i.e. the consciousness and behavior—of atomic particles and to relate electronics and atomics to human consciousness and behavior. Physicist John Archibald Wheeler's work suggests that the atomic nucleus can receive, remember, integrate and transmit information at extremely high-velocities and can probably engage in most of the basic social behavior that we observe in living organisms.

Interpersonal, emotional (i.e. motional), intellectual and social affairs at the electronic level and their transception by the nervous system define neuroelectronics.

Interpersonal, emotional, intellectual, and social events at the sub-atomic, nuclear level and their transception by the nervous system define neuroatomics.

Our understanding of atomic and nuclear processes has been limited by our language-logic-imagination-philosophy which tend to be Euclidean, Newtonian. We inevitably "psychologize" nature and personalize atomic events. Our laryngeal-muscular minds, imprinted in primitive childhood, cannot conceive of what we cannot conceive of; cannot experience what we have never experienced.

Exo-psychology views human destiny in terms of an evolving nervous system, designed by DNA intelligence (which uses planets as temporary embryonic nesting sites, in an interstellar migratory process destined to extend life-span, life-scope) to become symbiotic transceivers of astro-physical contelligence.

Our dialogue with DNA and our conversations with atomic-subatomic and astronomical energy signals must, however, be two-way. We must open our "minds" to receive the signals which are being sent to our nervous systems by DNA and by elemental intelligences. When we geneticize our psychology, i.e. think like DNA-RNA, we see the current human condition as a transient phase in the evolution of the nervous system. Since DNA creates us, it is logically diplomatic and theologically conventional (image of God) to base our psychology upon the laws and designs of molecular intelligence. Since the nucleus of the atom designs atoms and molecules, it is logical to base our psychology upon the laws and structures of nuclear physics and astronomy; to think of ourselves as "atoms" or even "stars" radiating, decaying, attracting, repelling, receiving and transmitting along frequency spectra, resonating, forming molecular social structures, possessing a characteristic electro-magnetic personality, moving through energy networks with relativistic focii, u.s.w.

Since our primitive psychological systems based on Newtonian geocentric principles have done little to enlighten or harmonize human philosophy, does it seem too fanciful to suggest that we should, in the future, base our psychological concepts on the laws and structures of physics, chemistry, and astronomy; and seek to explain human behavior in terms of natural rather than national inter-relatings?

Primitive, geo-centric, ego-centric, socio-centric psychology, ignoring the laws of bio-chemistry and physics, constructs a philosophy of mammalian emotions, Euclidean laryngeal-muscular symbols, and parochial values to explain "man and his universe."

Exo-psychology views human destiny in terms of an evolving nervous system, designed by DNA intelligence (which uses planets as temporary embryonic nesting sites in an interstellar migratory process destined to extend life-span, life-scope) to become symbiotic transceivers of astro-physical contelligence.

2. Exo-psychology (Psi-Phy) Is the Psychology of Physics: Philosophy Based on Scientific Fact

---

Indeed, there is some sociological evidence that science fictions are forcibly suppressed only when they are more likely to accelerate human evolution than the defensive orthodoxies which they challenge.

The theories presented in this transmission might be called Science Faction, or Philosophy of Science, or Psychology of Physics. Psi Phy.*

They are scientific in that they are based on empirical findings from physics, physiology, pharmacology, genetics, astronomy, behavioral psychology, and most important, neurology.

They are fictional in the Wittgensteinian sense that all theories and speculations beyond the mathematical propositions of natural science are subjective.

They are factional in the sense that current advances in Space Migration, Neurologic and the Life Extension sciences have already gone beyond the fantasies of most science fiction writers. Science Fact is now farther-out than Science Fiction. We are now creating a future which is more incredible than 2001. O'Neill space cylinders are more complex and advanced than Clarke-Kubrick space-ships.

This book was written in various prisons to which the author had been sentenced for dangerous ideology and violations of Newtonian laws.

Other philosophers (notably Christian theologians, statistical materialists, Marxian dialecticians) make different interpretations of the currently available corpus of scientific fact. Such theories, however popular, are equally fictional. History suggests that philosophies accepted as academic dogma or enforced by punitive legal sanctions are not necessarily any less fictional than those which are persecuted and censored. Indeed, there is some sociological evidence that science fictions are forcibly suppressed only when they are more likely to accelerate human evolution than the defensive orthodoxies which they challenge. We think of Socrates, Bruno, Copernicus, Darwin, Pasteur, Sakharov.

---

*"Everyone writes science fiction. . .but most write it without having the slightest idea that they are doing so." Joyce Carol Oates

. . .the species known as homo sapiens is evolving through an eight phase life-cycle. Four of these phases are designed for larval survival on the womb planet. The four more advanced phases are designed for survival and migration in interstellar space.

It gives us pleasure and increases our sense of freedom to believe that the species known as homo sapiens is evolving through an eight phase life-cycle. Four of these phases are designed for larval survival on the womb planet. The four more advanced phases are designed for survival and migration in interstellar space.

Exo-psychology is a theory of Interstellar Neurogenetics based on the following assumptions:

1.   There are millions of solar systems in our galaxy which have planets upon which organic life breeds and evolves.

2.   Since our planet is at the mid-point of the evolution of a G-type sun (five billion years) it is assumed that half of the planets in our galaxy upon which life is to be found are more advanced in the evolutionary sense than life on our planet.

3.   These more advanced cultures numbering, perhaps, in the millions, represent the future of our own evolution. They exist ahead of us in genetic time. "They" are "us" in the future.

4.   The same chemical elements and physical-chemical processes occur on all star systems in the known universe.

5.   Life as it exists on planet earth is not unique. We are as alike to our interstellar neighbors as "peas in a pod." ("We" in this cliche refers to all life forms on this planet.) We shall find only early and more advanced versions of ourselves. We are the alien life forms.

6.   Planets have a predictable life span. They are destroyed in the late "red-giant" phase of their suns. It is logical to suppose that Life migrates from planets before they are destroyed by aging suns or before their biological resources are exhausted.

7.   The Interstellar Neurogenetic theory suggests that Life is not designed to remain on the planet of birth, but to migrate throughout the galaxy.

8.   Life is seeded on young planets in the form of amino acid templates. These genetic blueprints contain the multi-billion year design of evolution. The basic tactics of evolution are metamorphosis and migration. We have been seeded on millions of other planets.

9.   The DNA code is literally a message outlining the course of evolution. On planet earth about half of this evolutionary blueprint has unfolded. The future half, blocked by histones, exists in quiescent form waiting to be activated—just as the chromosomes of a tadpole contain the future frog form. As the human embryo of four months contains the form of the neonate. Or the neonate the form of the pubescent teen-ager.

10.   The human species is now completing the fourth phase of its larval development. Think of the earth as a womb. Life so far on this planet is embryonic. When life leaves the planet it adopts post-fetal, post-larval existence.

The metamorphosis of human species from terrestrial to extra-terrestrial existence was signalled by the almost simultaneous discoveries of neuroactive drugs, electronic instruments, DNA structure, sub-atomic nuclear energies.

11.   It is convenient to describe larval life on earth as Newtonian—concerned with the gravity-bound mechanics of survival. And to describe extra-terrestrial existence as Einsteinian. Gravity selective.

The four Newtonian circuits of the nervous system are concerned with mastery of the four umbilical attitudes necessary for terrestrial survival.

      1. ventral-dorsal
      2. vertical (up-down)
      3. three-dimensional (left-right)
      4. protective-incorporative (for survival of the species)

The four Einsteinian circuits of the nervous system are designed for survival in post-terrestrial space and involve mastery of:

      5. the body as time-vehicle
      6. the nervous system as self-directed bio-electric computer
      7. the genetic code as molecular intelligence
      8. meta-physiological, nuclear-gravitational force-fields (quantum-mechanical)

12.   The metamorphosis of the human species from terrestrial to extra-terrestrial existence was signalled by the almost simultaneous discoveries of neuroactive drugs, electronic instruments, DNA structure, sub-atomic nuclear energies, quantum mechanics.

Each of the eight periods of individual human life involves gross alterations in morphology, behavior, physiology, and most important, neurology. In spite of the fact that these changes are obvious, even to the most untutored observer, the psychological-philosophic implications of these phases have not been understood by larval scientists and philosophers. This may be due to the possibility that the human species itself is evolving through the same eight phases and, until recently, has been almost exclusively preoccupied with the four basic, larval survival processes (vegetative, political, techno-logical, social).*

By analogy, a society of water-bound tadpoles would be neurologically inhibited from recognizing that the amphibious frog is a later version (both phylogenetically and individually) of itself.

The scientific facts about the nervous system, the creation of reality by imprint-ing, our position in the galaxy, neurotransmitter drugs, Einsteinian relativity, the DNA code—now available in any junior-college text—can be understood by an open-minded adolescent. These facts, however, are so alien to the Judeo-Christian-Marxist concep-tions of human nature that they have been repressed. Unconscious resistance to patent observations and scientific findings is a routine process in the evolution of human knowledge. We are familiar with the tendency to place under taboo facts which disturb orthodox religious dogmas. This taboo phenomenon is genetically determined. Prema-

The scientific facts about the nervous system, the creation of reality by imprinting, our position in the galaxy, neurotransmitter drugs, Einsteinian relativity, the DNA code—now available in any junior-college text—can be understood by an open-minded adolescent.

ture intimations of future metamorphosic stages would be dangerously confusing and demoralizing to a larval species.

Discovery of the serial imprinting capability of the nervous system, of bi-lateral (past-future) asymmetry in the cortex, the probability of advanced life forms on millions of planets in our local galaxy, and recognition of the longevity implications of the unused half of the DNA code, is producing a mutational quantum leap in the course of human evolution which is now preparing the species for migration from the planet.

---

*Rudimentary recognition of the larval, cyclical nature of contemporary human existence has been sporadically attained in earlier civilizations which have temporarily reached the necessary level of biological, political, technological, and reproductive security. In ancient China, India, Ceylon, Crete, Babylon, Greece, Islamic Damascus, Egypt, Renaissance Europe, a few neurologically elite, premature evolutes have used leisure (i.e. the time) and available technology to develop bodily hedonic, erotic, aesthetic expressions, science-fiction speculations and botanical methods of expanding neurological function beyond survival imprints.

At each chronological phase of individual evolution a new imprint is formed. Each imprint determines the positive and negative foci for subsequent conditioning of the newly activated circuit.

The human nervous system is evolving sequentially through eight maturational phases. At each phase a new circuit of the nervous system is activated and imprinted.

The four larval (neuro-umbilical) terrestrial circuits of the nervous system designed for attachment to and survival on earth are:

I.   The **Bio-survival Circuit**—mediating the reception, integration and transmission of neural signals concerned with cellular health and vegetative, metabolic security. Safety-danger.

II.   The **Emotion-locomotion Circuit**—mediating the reception, integration and transmission of neuro-muscular signals concerned with body-mobility, territorial control, and the avoidance of helplessness.

III.   The **Laryngeal-manual Dexterity Circuit**—mediating the reception, integration and transmission of neural signals from the nine laryngeal muscles and the hand which are concerned with language, artifacts and precise manipulatory movements.

IV.   The **Sexual-domestication Circuit**—mediating the reception, integration and transmission of neural signals concerned with sexual impersonation, courting, mating, parent-hood, child-rearing, and socialization.

The four circuits of the nervous system designed to mediate extra-terrestrial energies and to adapt to interstellar existence are:

V.   The **Neurosomatic Circuit**—mediating the reception, integration and transmission of sensory-somatic signals uncensored by larval imprints and designed to operate in a zero-gravity environment. Body consciousness.

VI.   The **Neuro-electric Circuit** which receives, integrates and transmits neural signals from all the other circuits and from the brain at the simultaneity and velocity of a bio-electric-grid; not programmed by survival imprints. Brain consciousness.

VII.   The **Neurogenetic Circuit** imprints the **DNA** code, receiving, integrating and transmitting **RNA** signals, thus operating at species-time, making possible biological immortality, and symbiosis with Higher Life forms. **DNA** consciousness.

VIII.   The **Metaphysiological-Neuro-atomic Circuit** is activated when the nervous system imprints sub-nuclear quantum-mechanical and gravitational signals, thus transcending biological existence. Quantum consciousness.

At each chronological phase of individual evolution a new imprint is formed. Each imprint determines the positive and negative foci for subsequent conditioning of the newly activated neural circuit. Each imprint defines a level of island reality. Recent-

Each imprint defines a level of island reality. Recently developed techniques for re-imprinting make possible serial, planful re-creation of realities.

ly developed techniques for re-imprinting make possible serial, planful re-creation of realities.

All the activity of the nervous system is based, of course, on chemical-electrical communication.

The first four larval circuits of the nervous system have been designed by the DNA code to deal with the Euclidian-Newtonian characteristics of the planet earth and the corollary asymmetries of human anatomy. The four later post-terrestrial circuits are designed for gravity-free psychosomatic reception, neuro-electric receptivity deciphering of DNA-RNA signals, and integration of sub-atomic messages.

5. There are Twenty-four Stages of Neural Evolution: Twelve Terrestrial and Twelve Extra-terrestrial*

The first twelve neurogenetic stages describe the evolution of life on this planet from single-celled organisms up to the most advanced insect and human societies and the development of the individual from birth through larval maturity, complete hive socialization.

In the preceding section we have defined eight periods of human evolution. Four are larval-terrestrial and four are designed for Space Migration.

The goal of evolution is Higher Intelligence—the sequential development of the nervous system—increasingly capable of receiving, integrating and transmitting a wider spectrum of signals of greater intensity, complexity and speed.

The more intelligent the species, the greater the capability of adapting and surviving. Bodies are the vehicles for transporting brains and seed. Bodies evolve to house and transport brains and sperm-ova more efficiently.

The genetic code has pre-programmed the nervous system to evolve in metamorphic stages. The basic strategies of evolution are metamorphosis and migration.

The sequential emergence of neural circuits in the individual human being recapitulates the phylogenetic appearance of nervous systems of greater complexity.

In studying neural activity and the evolution of nervous systems it becomes

---

*The book The Periodic Table of Evolution presents a systematic detailed discussion of the twenty-four stages of neuro-evolution—suggesting that biological and human-individual evolution is based on a blueprint design to be found in the Periodic Table of Chemical Elements.

This book treats the Periodic Table as a code-message which outlines the sequence of biological evolution and as a Rosetta stone from which the philosophic meaning of enduring human symbol-systems can be deciphered.

The neurogenetic symbol systems which can be understood in terms of the periodic table include:

> The Tarot
> The Zodiac
> The I Ching
> The playing card deck
> The Greco-Roman Olympic Pantheon
> The Hebrew Alphabet

These cultural games are seen as crude but generally accurate neuro-symbolic expressions by a pre-Einsteinian species of the basic model of galactic evolution which is based on the table of atomic elements. These "occult" systems are proto-scientific attempts to predict the course of evolution of life on and off the planet and can be seen as neuro-cultural communication systems in which humanity symbolizes natural laws.

Exo-psychology is a primer concerned with outlining the eight major sequences of neurological evolution. A detailed description of the 24 stages will be found in the subsequent volumes, The Periodic Table of Evolution and The Eight Calibre Brain, to which the interested reader is referred.

Chapter 5

The genetic code has pre-programmed the nervous system to evolve in metamorphic stages. The basic strategy of evolution is metamorphosis.

obvious that a three-part developmental sequence occurs.

Self-centered reception

Integration

Transmission-fusion

The neuron, which is the basic unit of biological contelligence, possesses three anatomical and functional divisions; the dendritic system which receives signals, the cell-body of the neuron which stores, integrates, interprets incoming signals and the axon which transmits the message. Each neuron, each circuit, and, indeed, the nervous system in its totality is divided into these three functions.

At the lowest level of unicellular and invertebrate life these three functions operate for the survival of the individual, but, at the higher stages of evolution, communication and fusions among members of species becomes more important for survival.

As each neural circuit emerges during the development of the individual, the self-oriented, receptive, input phase is the first to appear. The integrating phase follows and the organized transmission linking the organism to others is the third phase.

The development of the larval individual proceeds, therefore, through twelve phases (4 circuits x 3 orientations). Extra-terrestrial evolution also proceeds through twelve stages (4 x 3).

These twenty-four stages are both phylogenetic and ontological. The first twelve neurogenetic stages describe the evolution of life on this planet from single-celled organisms up to the most advanced insect and human societies and the development of the individual from birth through larval maturity, complete hive socialization.

A detailed description of these stages will be found in the books **The Eight Calibre Brain** and **The Periodic Table of Evolution.**

**This book attempts to present a complete philosophy of evolu-
tion. The perspective is post-terrestrial.**

This book attempts to present a complete philosophy of evolution. The perspective is post-terrestrial.

We assume (without extensive review or restatement) the current (1976) facts and
theories of nuclear physics, astronomy, DNA genetics, ethology, experimental imprinting, psycho-pharmacology, neurology and behavioral psychology.

Based on this consensus of scientific fact and on our extensive experimentation
with expanded and accelerated states of consciousness in the widest range of set,
setting and social context, we present:

1. A Bio-neural cosmology, a theory of the origin and evolution of life on and
off this planet.

2. A Neuro-muscular politic, defining the basic genetic dimensions of the free-
dom-control of muscular movement in territory.

3. A Neurogenetic epistemology, a theory defining the subjective True-False
and the consensual Fact-Error of laryngeal-manual (L.M.) symbol systems.

4. A Neurogenetic ethic, defining what is subjectively good-bad and consensually
right-wrong.

5. A Neurosomatic aesthetic, defining the natural, somatic dimensions of the
beautiful.

6. A Neurogenetic ontology, an anatomical-empirical theory of the eight levels
of reality, their evolution and interaction.

7. An Interstellar-Neurogenetic teleology, defining the future course of individual and species evolution, leading to longevity and galactic symbiosis with Higher forms
of life.

8. A Metaphysiological Neuro-atomic eschatology, predicting the imprinting of
the nervous system on to nuclear-gravitational-quantum force fields.

Higher Intelligence, located in interstellar nuclear-gravitational-quantum structures, has already sent a message to this planet. The U.F.O. message is in the form of the DNA code and of electro-atomic signals which can be transceived by the nervous system.

This book presents a neurogenetic cosmology—a theory of the origin, evolution and destiny of life on and off this planet.

This cosmology suggests that Higher Intelligence, located in interstellar nuclear-gravitational-quantum structures, has already sent a message to this planet. The U.F.O. message is in the form of the DNA code and of electro-atomic signals which can be transceived by the nervous system.

Life, a multi-billion year old unbroken energy-wire of evolving contelligence is the message.* Directed panspermia. Life was seeded on this womb-planet in the form of amino-acid templates designed to be activated by solar radiation and to unfold in a series of genetic molts and metamorphoses.

There are eight evolutionary phases which probably unfold on all oxygenated womb-planets in the galaxy.

The first four phases concern adaptation to the Newtonian characteristics of the womb-planet and are designed for fetal survival attached to the earth surface.

The four later phases are designed to decode, integrate and adapt to the Einsteinian electro-atomic-gravitational forces operating in post-terrestrial space.

The first four phases are muscular-material and define tiny survival "island realities" to which the organism is attached.

The four post-larval phases are designed to propel and maintain life off this planet.

The biological "master plan" of organic evolution located in DNA directs the unfolding of the circuits of the nervous system.

One major goal of life is to become Increasingly Intelligent (I^2) in order to decode somatic signals within the body, within the nervous system itself, signals from the DNA code and metaphysiological neuro-atomic energy patterns.

The history of life and of humanity is best defined in terms of the evolution of the nervous system, of contelligence. In place of anthropological categories based on geography (Java Man), adaptive behavior (Neolithic Man), we suggest the following periods of neural evolution. Each period is considered as larval or robot to the subsequent.

1. Unicellular-invertebrate phase (marine): approach-avoidance for vegetative survival.

2. Vertebrate animal phase: territorial dominance and mastery of gravity.

3. Humanoid phase: precise-dexterous nervous system for Laryngeal-Manual (L.M.) symbol manipulation.

---

*In place of the word "intelligence," exo-psychology prefers the word "contelligence," referring to the reception (consciousness), integration and transmission of energy signals. There are eight levels of contelligence.

Each life form on this planet is an alien immigrant from outer space. We are all Unidentified Flying Organisms.

4. Human phase: nervous system imprinted for sexual-domestic role allowing for division of labor, caste, class, custom. For species survival.

5. Neurosomatic phase: insightful control of the gravity-free body. Body consciousness.

6. Neuroelectric Phase: insightful control of the nervous system detached from somatic programs. Brain consciousness.

7. Neurogenetic phase: insightful communication between the nervous system and the DNA code leading to symbiosis and Life Extension. DNA consciousness.

8. Metaphysiological neuro-atomic phase: insightful communication between the nervous system and sub-nuclear energy. Quantum consciousness.

Each life form on this planet is an alien immigrant from outer space. We are all Unidentified Flying Organisms.

During the first four larval phases the emphasis is on attachment to the earth-womb for survival in one-G space. During the four later phases the emphasis is on interstellar survival;

5. management of the body as zero-gravity vehicle

6. mastery of the nervous system as transceiver of high-speed bio-electric signals

7. symbiotic DNA linkage with other galactic life forms

8. transfusion with metaphysiological intelligence.

These eight neurological phases of evolution listed here are discussed in the book, **The Eight Calibre Brain.** It is important to note that an evolutionary, galaxy-centered cosmology and teleology (theology, if you will) is being presented. It is necessarily Psi-Phy in flavor. There is no dogmatic commitment to the metaphor. It is one hypothetical, cosmological model, based upon current scientific facts from psychology, ethology, genetics, neurology, and astro-physics; one model to explain the origin and meaning of life and to predict future evolution in a context in which current human forms are seen as larval, fetal.

Cosmology is traditionally considered a "far out," risky enterprise, inevitably involving the sort of speculation that makes people uneasy. There is, indeed, a taboo censoring teleological discussions. This future-terror (Neophobia) often leads to inquisitorial repression. Bruno was burned at the stake for persisting in cosmological broadcasts, for raising embarrassing futique questions. In his essay **On the Infinite Universe and the Worlds** Bruno presents this probing dialogue:

Elpino: How is it possible that the universe be infinite?

Philotheo: How is it possible that the universe be finite?

Elpino: How do you claim that you can demonstrate this infinitude?

Philotheo: Do you claim that you can demonstrate this finitude?

Elpino: What is this spreading forth?

Philotheo: What is this limit?

A dreadful malaise has demoralized the modern world. Spenglerian doom. This crisis is not political, ecological, energetic or economic. It is philosophic. Pre-partum depression.

The creative cosmologist presents Hir* theory and then asks the critic to explicate Hir own. And here is the tender point. Although every larval bases Hir life on an implicit cosmology (usually vague dogmas imprinted on the childhood nervous system) most practical people are reluctant to verbalize their basic beliefs, because they do not stand the scrutiny of rational view and scientific perspective:

Larval Philosopher: How can you claim that the human being is a larval form of a future metamorphosed entity of higher intelligence and consciousness?

Exo-Psychologist: How can you claim that evolution stopped with the present human nervous system?

Larval Philosopher: It is absurd to speculate about a Higher Intelligence seeding earth with pre-programmed genetic blueprints.

Exo-Psychologist: What is your theory of the origin of life? Old Testament Genesis? Chance and statistical probability? Lightening bolts triggering life in methane-ammonia puddles? i.e., spontaneous generation?

A dreadful malaise has demoralized the modern world. Spenglerian doom. This crisis is not political, ecological, energetic or economic. It is philosophic. Pre-partum depression. Technological, economic and political conferences are inevitably pessimistic because they avoid the real issues, the gyroscopic-navigational questions: Why are we here and where are we going?

Cosmological questions about origins are intimately linked to theories of destinations.

Speculations about the origin of life provide the foundation (conscious or unconscious) of every human culture. Inevitably questions about

Who did it and why?

lead to answers about how we can get to where we are supposed to go. If Allah did it, then we are en route to Allah. If no one did it then we are going nowhere.

Since each of the eight circuits of the nervous system produces its own reality, each imprint naturally provides its own answers limited to the imprint.

Circuit 1, for example, defines the goal of life in viscerotonic, vegetative, cellular survival terms—to eat, drink, breathe, avoid pain, danger and cold. And so it goes for the other larval levels of reality.

*In this transmission the union of male-female is taken for granted as a neurogenetic necessity. The general terms "man/Mankind" are never used. We employ the word SHe to refer to the generic post-terrestrial human. The generic possessive is Hir, i.e. a combination of "his" and "her."

Most evolutionists rely on chance as the determining factor and attribute the apparent ascendency of humanity upon the fortuitous accidental emergence of the unique nervous system.

At this critical time in history there are two broad approaches to the questions of Why? Where from? Where to? and By whom?

Evolutionists Larval Scientists

Creationists Larval Theologians

The "issue" is complicated by the fact that science and theology are inextricably linked and that many scientific evolutionists are closet creationists.

The currently orthodox "scientific" theory of evolution holds that all plants and animals have developed from inorganic molecules, stewing in the Pre-Cambrian slime, sparked into life by electro-magnetic processes three billion years ago; that chance and natural selection working slowly but relentlessly with nucleic acid chains have produced the variety and complexity of biological life. Most evolutionists believe that all life forms derive from a common origin because of the amazing similarity of DNA among species and because of the apparent continuity of phylogenetic and individual development.

Evolutionists who propose this "chance-slime" theory tend to be atheistic, scientific, skeptical and pessimistic about the existence of human-type life on other planets. They tend to remain silent about the possible existence of Higher Intelligence in the galaxy. G. G. Simpson, a leading evolutionary philosopher, has cited the statistical improbability of life evolving on other planets the way it has unfolded on earth. To strict statistical evolutionists the emergence of human-type life, even on this planet, is improbable, if not impossible.

Most evolutionists rely on chance as the determining factor and attribute the apparent ascendency of humanity upon the fortuitous accidental emergence of the unique nervous system.

Creationists vary in kind and species as widely as do evolutionists, but in general they believe that at some early period of history distinct species were separately created by a Higher Intelligence called Yahweh, Jehovah, God, Allah, u.s.w.

Many creationists rely upon the biblical Genesis which states that God created the various kinds of animals, that "man" was created separately and "women" as an afterthought.

Sophisticated forms of Creationism have been produced by scientists such as Carolus Linnaeus, the Father of Taxonomy, who claimed, "there are just so many species as there were forms created in the beginning." Louis Agassiz, a Harvard biologist, declared that the Creator designed the living forms we now witness.

A basic difference between these two points of view is this:

Evolutionists believe that the complex variety came from the simple.

Creationists believe that the complexity and variety were designed from the origin.

It is interesting that few, if any, thinkers from either camp have emphasized the possibility of evolution continuing or speculated in any detail on the specific forms that the future may provide.

Evolutionists also tend to believe in the "accidental," chance nature of the process and to avoid the notion of a pre-destined design or designing intelligence.

Creationists have tended to be orthodox religionists who personalize the Divine Creator and tend to place humanity on the apex of terrestrial life—usually allowing for a post-mortem, post-biological existence for chosen believers. Some theologies provide for extra-terrestrial, metaphysiological entities—demons, angels, devils, Saints. An unbridgeable gulf has developed between theological creationists and scientific evolutionists who can find no evidence for the celestial fantasies and wishful immortalities of the former.

It is interesting that few, if any, thinkers from either camp have emphasized the possibility of evolution continuing or speculated in any detail on the specific forms that the future may provide. The existence of Advanced Forms of Intelligence on other planets or in humanity's future is particularly embarrassing to scientists who have, perhaps, been scared-off by the celestial absurdities of religious orthodoxies.

Exo-psychology presumes to offer new solutions to these classic questions by suggesting:
1. that life on this planet is not unique
2. that the planet has been seeded
3. that evolution of the various species unfolds on all biological planets according to the same pre-determined plan
4. that life is designed to migrate from the nursery planet
5. the great mutations are pre-programmed to appear in our future.

Exo-psychology attempts to assemble evidence from all the sciences, to pay respectful attention to the enduring myths which bubble up from the nervous systems of the past—and to make practical extrapolations from both sources of data to anticipate the future.

It is thus possible to entertain a Creative-Evolutionism which holds that the original amino-acid templates had built into their design:
1. standard physiological and anatomical methods for creating and dealing with the various environmental challenges which coincidentally-evolve on planets like ours
2. pre-determined sequences of improvements in anatomy and particularly in neurology which allow evolving species to metamorphize to a point where they can leave the planet.

It is not necessary to accept "directed panspermia" to assume this exo-psychological point-of-view. The most conservative scientific logic leads to the future probability of:

improvements in the use of the nervous system
genetic engineering
concomitant variations in human stock
extra-planetary colonization.

If a credible, respectable God does not exist, let us by all means invent Hir. We do need someone interesting to talk to.

Science fiction has developed into a popular form of literature. The best of Sci-Fi becomes Psi-Phy, the Psychology of Physics. Television and movies also reflect a growing interest in the mutated future. It is of interest, however, that few science-fiction writers are capable of imagining Higher Intelligence. This inability to specify a harmonious and successful future is due to the nature of the nervous system. Caterpillars cannot write with convincing reality about post-larval life.

Since the "head revolution" of the 1960's, the basic principles of neuro-logic and reality-change have been widely accepted. While the terms **imprinting, serial-imprinting** and **re-imprinting** are not often used, there is growing "hip" acceptance of the notion that each nervous system creates its own reality. The vulgar, even cynical, reaction to this ontological discovery is to smile tolerantly and say, "Everyone is crazy in their own way." "Do your own thing." "Don't lay your trip on me."

The next neurological step is to accept the responsibility and say, "Since our imprints create reality, let us choose realities which are as fantastic and thrilling as possible. Almost anything we can conceive, we can make real."

If exo-psychology can imagine human intelligence expanding to extra-terrestrial dimensions, is it not neurologically possible to real-ize these challenging possibilities? If we can imagine directed pan-spermia, then it can exist. Indeed, we can do it ourselves. If Higher Intelligence has not seeded space, then there is no reason why we cannot do it. Agriculture is, after all, "directed spermia."

Here the polarities of the Evolutionists and Creationists can be harmonized. Our geneticists can help humanity become the Creator of Species, on this planet and, via interstellar migration, in space.

Humans have always created God in their own image. Neurogenetics now makes it possible for humanity:

1. To contact Higher Intelligence which may have designed the evolutionary sequence, or
2. To design the evolutionary process so as to create Higher Intelligence.

If a credible, respectable God does not exist, let us by all means invent Hir. We do need someone to talk to.

At the present time, these are simply educated speculations about the future. But it does seem probable that our micro-hopes and tele-hopes can create the realities to come.

Exo-psychology predicts that the Higher Intelligence is to be found within the micro-physiology of the DNA code and suggests that the most interesting way to use our time is to attempt to contact the Higher Intelligence and to hope that our neurons and amino-acids are capable of fusion with Hir.

Politics is the externalization of emotions; mammalian, musculotonic behavior mediated by the emergency (sympathetic) nervous system to seize or defend territory.

Towards the end of the sixteenth century, Giordano Bruno aroused the groggy world, asking it to fling its mind far beyond the planets. He speculated that the cosmos extended to infinity—without an edge.

This is itself was not so shocking; but Bruno went considerably further—he postulated a multiplicity of worlds; suns and planets with life, unseen companions for the race of man. He toyed with man's conception of himself; for this, and for magical claims and political entanglements, he was burned in 1600.

Charles A. Whitney

Politics is the externalization of emotions; mammalian, musculotonic behavior mediated by the emergency (sympathetic) nervous system to seize or defend territory.

There are four levels of terrestrial freedom, four conditions of servitude, four levels of social fusion all related to the basic mammalian mesomorphic drive to get "on Top." There are also four neurological freedoms which characterize post-terrestrial existence.

1. **Biological, Viscerotonic Freedom** to protect one's life and health and the Constraint of actions which threaten the cellular survival of others. Personal health. Public health. Access to vital supplies. Expression and control of violence.

2. **The Territorial Freedom** to maintain one's living space and to move freely; the Constraint of intrusion on the living space of another or the control of the mobility of others.

3. **Technological Cerebrotonic Freedom** to manufacture, possess and use artifacts and to transmit symbols. The Constraint of using force to take the artifacts of others or to censor their symbol systems.*

4. **The Cultural Freedom** to select one's life style and socio-sexual role. The Constraint of interfering with the courtship styles, mating rites, impersonation styles, and domestic mores of others.

These basic larval Freedoms and Constraints define the muscular politics of material, Newtonian, terrestrial One-gravity existence.

Next we consider the politics of time.

The politics of extra-terrestrial, Einsteinian existence concern the Freedom and

---

*This book is being written in prison under the well-publicized threat of assassination by extremists of both left and right. This manuscript has, at best, an even chance of getting published. Exo-psychology is not an armchair philosophy of abstractions; it has been forged in the dangerous realities of larval existence on this planet.

The politics of extra-terrestrial, Einsteinian existence concern the Freedom and Control of energies within the human body, within the structure of the atom.

Control of energies within the human body, within the nervous system, within the DNA code, and within the structure of the atom.

5. **Somatic Freedom** to control one's own body function and sensory input. The Constraint of interfering with another's bodily function or sensory intake. The Constraint of imposing involuntary stimuli on others. Specifically this implies the freedom to ingest any drug or food and use any erotic stimulation one wishes and the Constraint from drugging, torturing or erotically stimulating others without their consent.

6. **Neurophysical Freedom** to expand, accelerate, control one's own nervous system and to broadcast and receive electronically. The Freedom to migrate from the planet. The Constraint of interfering with the brain-reward processes and the neuro-electrical transception of others. The Constraint of interfering with the extra-planetary plans of others.

7. **The Genetic Freedom** of all life forms to live and evolve into symbiotic fusions. The Constraint of actions which threaten the evolution of other life forms. Specifically this implies the freedom to conduct genetic research; to facilitate one's own evolution and symbiosis. And the Constraint of genetic research which hurts, manipulates, enslaves or genocides other life-forms.

8. **The Nuclear Freedom** of all life forms to attain fusion with metaphysiological intelligence; to conduct nuclear particle research. The Constraint of actions which use nuclear energy to threaten the lives and evolution of other life forms.

Exo-psychology defines eight levels of Revolution-revelation:*

8. Nuclear Revelation (quantum time)
7. Genetic Revelation (DNA time)
6. Electronic Revelation (brain time)
5. Hedonic Revelation (body time)
4. Cultural-sexual Revolution (hive-domestication power)
3. Technological Revolution (mechanical power)
2. Political Revolution (musculotonic power)
1. Violence Revolution (viscerotonic power)

*Revolution is change or mutation in material externals. Revelation is change or mutation in neurological-extra-terrestrial energies. **Revolution without revelation is tyranny; revelation without revolution is slavery.**

Chapter 8

These basic larval Freedoms and Constraints define the muscular
politics of material, Newtonian, terrestrial One-gravity existence.

Exo-psychology also defines eight social groupings:

8. Fusion with nuclear structure
7. Symbiosis
6. Telepathy; cyborg fusion
5. Somatic fusion; tantra, nature communes, space colonies
4. Cultural-ethical groupings (hive, tribe)
3. Technical-professional-occupational groupings
2. Political-territorial groupings
1. Bio-survival groupings; military-medical

Each nervous system creates its own island realities. Truth is defined by the wiring of the individual nervous system—genetic, imprinted and conditioned.

This book presents a neurogenetic epistemology—a theory of what is subjectively true and what is consensually factual.

There are eight levels of truth.

1.   Bio-survival viscerotonic truth: the neural signals mediated by the First Circuit which define vegetative-cellular safety and danger. (My toothache.)

2.   Emotion-locomotion truth: the neural signals mediated by the Second Musculotonic Circuit which define territorial status—dominance-helplessness. (My emotion.)

3.   L.M. Symbolic Cerebrotonic truth: the neural signals mediated by the laryngeal-manual Third Circuit which discriminate and connect my artifacts and my symbols.

4.   Cultural-domestic truth: the neural signals mediated by the Fourth Circuit imprint which define soc-sex role. (My socio-sexual values.)

5.   Neurosomatic truth: somatic-sensory signals, free of larval-survival cues, directly registered and mediated by the Fifth Circuit. (My pleasure, my beauty.)

6.   Neurophysical truth: all the neural signals registered as bio-electric impulses received by the brain. (My synaptic transmissions.)

7.   Neurogenetic truth: signals sent by DNA-RNA to the brain. (My DNA memories and forecasts.)

8.   Neuro-atomic truth; atomic-nuclear-quantum signals registered and mediated by the brain.

Each nervous system creates its own island realities. Truth is defined by the wiring of the individual nervous system—genetic, imprinted and conditioned. The "fact" is that the human brain deals with a reality of several billion signals a minute—changing patterns of vibrations—mediated by the eight circuits. Whatever interpretations the individual's imprinted-conditioned symbol systems impose on these energies is "true"— although it may not be "true" for others. John's First Circuit toothache is the Dentist's Third Circuit "clinical problem."

Children imprint the survival cellular tastes, the emotional muscular reflexes, the L.M. symbols and the soc-sex models of their parent-culture. This socialization of larval imprints and conditionings makes consensual communication possible. The island-realities of the child overlap the island realities of the parents and the local tribal group. The child learns the movements of the laryngeal muscles and the manual muscles that create the appropriate symbols. Epistemological games are thus learned. These social reality-islands contain names for labelling energy clusters and relating them. The L.M. symbols, labels and learned sequences of association are assigned "factual" semantic meaning. Facts exist only within the limited framework of the parochial game. Social reality-islands set up criteria for determining fact and error, right and wrong, which may or may not have any relationship to what is experienced by the individual as "true" or "false."

Virtue and Sin are consensual-social. Each cultural group sets up its rules for virtuous behavior, sanctifies actions which contribute to the preservation of the hive.

There are 12 larval soc-sex roles which can be imprinted by either male or female.* These roles are valued as consensually "virtuous" or "sinful" depending on their meaning to the domestication-style of the society and its sub-cultures. These roles are valued subjectively as "good" or "bad" on the basis of the Fourth-Circuit imprint.

The Fourth Circuit imprint, determined by genetic sexual-templating and the accidental proximities of adolescence, determines domesticated sex role. The style and object of gender expression-inhibition, sexual impersonation. "Good" is what triggers off the imprinted sexual response. "Good" is what excites and attracts; causes the sexual-domestic juices to flow. "Good" is what provokes the experience—"Ah, there! Now I am at home!" This can be genital penetration-incorporation. It can be parental, protective contact. It can be reception of signals indicating collective security, social approval, applause, patriotic symbols. It can be sado-masochistic contact. It can be laryngeal-manual rhythmic fusions. "Bad" is what turns-off or threatens a soc-sexual reward. To the domesticated primate (human), "good" and "bad" are subjective sexual expressions (genital, parental or sublimated-displaced). Usually secret, often unconscious.

Virtue and Sin are consensual-social. Each cultural group sets up its rules for virtuous behavior, sanctifies actions which contribute to the preservation of the hive. Society is based on the control and direction of socio-sexual behavior. The particular soc-sex virtues of the group—emotional, symbolic, and stylistic—are usually determined early in the group's history by dominant leaders who impose their fourth imprint sexual eccentricities on the culture. St. Paul didn't like women. Mohammed was polygamous-exploitive. Luther was paternal. Since most modern societies have been codified by menopausal, power-oriented men, the moral systems tend to be prudish, exploitive and chauvinistic. Social reponsibilities thus determine virtue and sin—which are always sexual in origin.

The relationship among the 12 sex roles is the basis of civilization.

Various sub-cultures sanctify certain soc-sex roles and proscribe others, building elaborate ethical codes around the predilections of the mammalian politicians who seize power.

Disastrous personal and social conflicts (guilt, shame) occur because the subjective, private "good" does not usually coincide with soc-sex "virtue."

---

*These 12 roles are also stages of development, described in Part II of this Manual. While each human evolves through these 12 stages in the course of individual development—each of us is genetically programmed to emphasize one of the 12 roles which, when interfaced, make up the 12-element human-social molecule.

When the "mind" discovers that the "body" is a polymorphous, psychosomatic Zen-pleasure-laboratory designed for zero-gravity floating, with trillions of cells merrily copulating every second, imprinted rewards seem pale, static, and second-hand.

There are eight levels of pleasure. The four larval circuits provide rewarding, reassuring signals that the survival lines to the island-realities are secure. The four post-larval pleasures come from direct awareness of natural energy signals—the biological equipment, freed from larval imprint, harmoniously mediating natural energies.

This book presents a neurological Zen-aesthetic—defining beauty as natural. Natural as beauty. Here again we distinguish between subjective-psychosomatic pleasure and imprinted-learned reward.

The first four circuits limit consciousness to the wiring of the imprinted and conditioned, and focus upon what is physically, emotionally, mentally and socially rewarding. The larval body is imprint-wired and trained to perform goal-directed game-oriented robot sequences in Newtonian space. The billions of signals per minute which flood into the nervous system from the body and its sense receptors are censored from awareness, tuned out from consciousness at a brain-stem reflex level. The survival tactic is obvious. The body is a trillion-cell, poly-organ bio-survival instrument. If the four-brained individual tunes into the myriad symphonic waves of polymorphous signalry flashed by the senses, SHe could not attend to larval survival responsibilities.

The brain, of course, "knows" every precise detail about the anatomy and physiology of the body and monitors millions of signals per second, but the larval-robot mind is "slave-wired" to reflex reaction, unable to decipher or consciously control its own equipment.

Each of the four larval circuits has its imprinted reward-pain cues which are limited and stereotyped: food preferences, emotional cues, L.M. symbolic reflexes, sexual-domestic comforts. When the "mind" discovers that the "body" is a polymorphous, psychosomatic Zen-pleasure-laboratory designed for zero-gravity floating, with trillions of cells merrily copulating every second, imprinted rewards seem pale, static, and second-hand. The activating of "natural body consciousness" is a dramatic step in evolution. The Hedonic Resurrection of the Body is the first step towards extra-terrestrial existence, a profound philosophic discovery, none the less "spiritual" because it occurs in the context of anti-social hedonic behavior, forbidden to the domesticated terrestrial.

We have called this emergence of the Fifth Circuit a "hurtling of the hedonic gap." With the four neuro-umbilical lines retracted, the "mind" discovers that the "natural is the beautiful," that the source of intensified pleasure is somatic function, that there is no social reward or terrestrial gratification which can compare with body consciousness. We have called the Zen experience of the Fifth, somatic Circuit rapture. The body freed from terrestrial attachments, ready to navigate in the zero-gravity of interstellar existence.

The existence of the Fifth Circuit and the natural rapture experience has always

Humans would be well advised to treat each other gently at this stage in evolution because mutation is a time of uncertainty and fragility. Indeed, since the individual recapitulates evolution in Hir own life it would be helpful if, at each larval stage, the child were given accurate information about the neurological changes that are occurring. The facts of metamorphosis explained.

been a taboo topic proscribed by larval social law because it is instinctively recognized that if the human being discovers a source of pleasure and revelation within Hir body, the commitment and dedication to terrestrial social rewards will diminish. This is the genetic predisposition to escape from the social imprints. Historically it is no accident that the aesthetic, rapturous experience was accepted by affluent aristocracies who are "above and beyond" social sanctions.

We have seen that each neural circuit as it emerges tends to regard the preceding stage as immature. The suckling infant is immature to the walking child. The post-pubescent flushed with the new experiences and secret discoveries of the "boy-girl-game" looks with amused tolerant scorn at the symbol-manipulations of the pre-adolescent.

It is also true that each of the imprinted "minds" looks with anxious disapproval upon newly emerging realities which tend to disrupt its stability.

We speak here of "neurogenetic politics." Metamorphic chauvinism. The transition periods in the individual's growth, as new circuits emerge, are stormy, unsettling, and vulnerable. It is well-known that adolescence is such a period of sturm und drang. The emergence of a new person, a new tunnel-reality-identity, is based on complex bio-chemical changes, intricate new live-wiring of millions of neural fibres, the development of and taking-over by higher neural centers, the ascendance of new imprints, and new bio-electrical patterns. The fragility of these neuro-umbilical transitions is not well understood. The passage from a First Circuit state, with its emphasis on passive security, to the second state of mobility and power exposes the nervous system to frightening vulnerability. The babe leaves the mother's arms to face the play yard. The adolescent facing with a newly-activated sexual body the pressure to develop a social identity.

The delicacy of this process and the permanence of the new imprint "fix" is both awesome and awe-full. A new person is created as each circuit of the nervous system emerges.

The new extensions of the reality-island must be hooked up without disturbing the earlier "realities." The new "person" must be integrated.

The human being is at present a confused, frightened, embryonic creature, mutating from Circuit 4 to Circuit 5, from terrestrial to extra-terrestrial existence. Humans would be well advised to treat each other gently at this stage in evolution because mutation is a time of uncertainty and fragility. Indeed, since the individual recapitulates evolution in Hir own life it would be helpful if, at each larval stage, the child were given accurate information about the neurological changes that are occurring. The facts of metamorphosis explained.

Unfortunately the different demands of the different imprints are externalized as politics, dogma and ethics. Neurological differences "exstitutionalized" as social

Just as blossom follows bud so does virtuous republic (Stage 11) become centralized empire (Stage 12) and empire flower into somatic hedonism (Stage 13). It is to slow this trend that the socialisms ban rock-and-roll.

conflicts. The dread which the child and the larval adult feels in response to the pressure to change, the suspicion of different conceptions of reality, the inability to adapt to change, are caused by the most basic larval insecurity—a loosening of the neuro-umbilical imprint connections.

The transition from the Fourth to the Fifth Circuit is complicated because it has been viewed as anti-social. The perils of hedonism! The socially dangerous discovery of the rapture circuit: "My natural bodily sensations are more pleasurable and more interesting than territorial social-rewards. I want to stay loose and high. Mundane affairs are robot."

During the 1960's both Presidents Johnson and Nixon clearly recognized that the American work-aesthetic was threatened by hedonism. While young men lost interest in fighting on far-flung foreign shores, ominous comparisons were made in State of the Union speeches to the "fall of the Roman Empire." The misguided implications were that Hedonism corrupted the Empire and, that if Decadence could be checked, the Empire would continue expanding.

The static moralism of Johnson-Nixon fails to perceive the evolutionary cyclical nature of history. Just as blossom follows bud so does virtuous republic (Stage 11) become centralized empire (Stage 12) and empire flower into somatic hedonism (Stage 13). It is to slow this trend that the socialisms ban rock-and-roll.

In the past, hedonism invariably led to the collapse of empire. Imperial capture could not compete with private rapture. Hedonism has, therefore, never been recognized by larval historians as an evolutionary advance, but as a social threat. When the somatic nervous system can be attached to and detached from larval imprints at will the first step away from imprinted-robothood has been taken. The Fifth brain begins to transceive directly the first language of nature—the metacultural biochemistry of the body. When the individual begins to attain control of neurosomatic function, can dial and tune the pleasures of the body, SHe is taking the first step towards control of the nervous system.

In the book **The Principles and Practice of Hedonic Psychology,*** a crude attempt was made to encourage a science of neurosomatics, a systematic study of the psychology of pleasure. Hedonics is not an end-point, but must be seen as a transitional phase in the evolution towards extra-terrestrial existence.

The emergence of Hedonic Psychology in the 1960's was greeted with official scorn and persecution. Larval politicians correctly saw the cultural perils of hedonism. The neurosomatic perspective frees the human from addiction to hive rewards (which are now seen as robot) and opens up vistas of natural satisfaction and meta-social

Abstracted in the January 1973 issue of **Psychology Today.**

SPACE MIGRATION   INTELLIGENCE INCREASE   LIFE EXTENSION

Bodily revelation has been routinely condemned as immoral by every larval social-ethical system at the same time it has been eloquently praised by those aesthetes who have tuned into the somatic network.

aesthetic revelation. The revelation is this: "I can learn to control internal, somatic function, to select, dial, tune incoming stimuli, not on the basis of security, power, success, or social responsibility, but in terms of aesthetics and psychosomatic wisdom. To feel good. To escape from terrestrial pulls."

Since the Neurological sixties we have seen an efflorescence of consumer sensuality and body interest. Massage, sensory awakening, yoga, martial art, diet, health-food-fads, erotic performance. The "new hedonics" is a manifestation of the first beginnings of Circuit 5 Zen Consciousness.

The triggering causative factor in this Fifth Circuit mutation was, of course, the discovery of neuro-somatic drugs. In the 1960's people in technological societies discovered that neuro-somatic chemicals "turn-on" the body and provide escape from mundane reality-islands. The moment of this discovery is, for most, en ethical detonation. Bodily revelation has been routinely condemned as immoral by every larval social-ethical system at the same time it has been eloquently praised by those aesthetes who have tuned into the somatic network. But the problem of neurosomatic rapture is that it is a post-larval reaction, and has mixed survival value for terrestrial existence.

The ability to receive, integrate, and transmit somatic sensations, to control the body as time-ship, is necessary in extraplanetary existence but can be a dangerous distraction for mundane life. The drug culture of the 1960's produced millions of enraptured hedonists, Hippies, sensualists, nature-lovers floating free of social ties but with no place to go. Some Zen philosophers cynically make a virtue out of this navigational uncertainty. Werner Erhart, for example, glorifying the meaningless of life.

Activation of the Fifth Circuit marks the infancy of interstellar existence. Hippies and Zen adepts are grounded butterflies, neurologically ready but technologically unprepared for flight. Instead of being hailed as harmless heralds of a mutation to come, they were predictably derogated and forced underground.

Musicians, poets, artists, aesthetes have traditionally been the exponents of neurosomatic consciousness and of drugs which enhance sensory experience because the Fifth Circuit defines the aesthetic level of reality. The Einsteinian relativity of direct sensuality, of the natural. The Zen insight. "That's the way it is: beautiful."

Beauty lies in the neurosomatic "I" of the beholder.

Each circuit of the nervous system has its own imprinted criterion for "pleasant" or "rewarding." At Circuit 1 Mother's apron or the gun can be pleasant. Safety is beautiful. Circuit 2 welcomes stimuli promising dominance and mobility. At Circuit 3 L.M. symbolic rewards appear beautiful. A hundred dollar bill. At Circuit 4 there is the sperm-egg stimulus—"the girl's underpants" memorialized by Kurt Vonnegut. These positive cues are sought for their imprint-conditioned reward and not for the aesthetic pleasure of the natural "seen" as it is.

Larval reward-pleasure has been institutionalized in the form of "show-business"

In advanced civilizations of the past, the Fifth Circuit was attained by adepts and hedonists who created the disciplined tradition of sensual-delight. Somatic art is the Zen aesthetic of the naked-natural. Direct stimulus by-passing symbols. Neurosomatic art gets the body high.

and social "art." The skillful artist unconsciously selects the stimuli which social conditioning has associated with safe-dangerous, powerful-weak, competent-stupid and sexually arousing. The criteria for what is considered artistically successful are stylized, socially conditioned, learned in terms of larval symbols. Fifth Circuit rapture, however, is the response of the sense organs to natural stimulation, divorced from terrestrial conditioned meaning.

In advanced civilizations of the past, the Fifth Circuit was attained by adepts and hedonists who created the disciplined tradition of sensual-delight. Somatic art is the Zen aesthetic of the naked-natural. Direct stimulus by-passing symbols. Neurosomatic art gets the body high.

The origin of much social art is somebody's neurosomatic signal which has been socialized—imprinted and learned as "artistic."

At the present time our scientific knowledge of bodily function combined with our technical affluence (especially birth control devices) has brought us to a point of Fifth Circuit breakthrough. Humans are devoting more time to body-consciousness, learning how to tune into somatic conversations, master somatic yogas which provide precise control of bodily function.

However, beauty and rapture are not evolutionary ends in themselves, but anticipatory preparations on the part of a neurogenetically evolving species for extra-planetary existence.

Consciousness is defined as energy received by structure. Intelligence is defined as energy transmitted by structure. For the human being the structures are neural circuits and their anatomical connections.

This book presents a neurogenetic ontology—a theory of eight levels of reality and their interaction.

All realities are neurological—patterns of impulses received, stored and transmitted by neural structures. Consciousness is defined as energy received by structure. Intelligence is defined as energy transmitted by structure. For the human being the structures are neural circuits and their anatomical connections. Please re-read the last three sentences.

For thousands of years ontologists have speculated futilely about the nature of reality. There can be no more room for debate. Surely the nervous system determines every aspect of human reality. What is "real" is what is registered by nerve endings, coded in neural memory banks, and transmitted by nerve fibres.

The ontological question is so easily resolved we wonder why there was ever any confusion. After all, the circulation of the blood was understood four centuries ago. The structure of the nervous system, the fibrous wiring of the sense organs, and the connections to the brain are so anatomically obvious that one is puzzled at the inability of earlier anatomists and physiologists to understand that the nervous system is the seat of consciousness and thus the solution of many ontological questions that have vexed and confused man's thinking. We face here, perhaps, another contrived, deliberate stupidity, a protective myopia, a species taboo which shrouds attempts to explain consciousness and intelligence-expanding processes. The facts about the nervous system are too robot embarrassing, too challenging to larval theological and political systems. It is just too early on the evolutionary clock for the species to face the neurological facts, for the robots to decipher their own circuitry.

Consider the sad fate of Julien Offray de Lamettrie, whose futique genius caused him to be dismissed from his medical posts and exiled to Holland:

> Lamettrie demonstrated by comparative methods the relationship between man and other living beings, and proceeded to a theory of the evolution of organisms. He stated that psychical life is observable already on the lowest level of evolution. **Investigating the functions of the brain, Lamettrie tried to discern various stages of its formation which are of primary importance in the development of mental life.** Also he protested against an evaluation of the moral character of men which depends on the acceptance of religious doctrines. Although Lamettrie was described as a crude materialist, he also influenced idealist philosophers.
>
> This 'scapegoat of 18th century materialism' has been blamed and despised by many who had not read a single page of his books.
>
> He is best known for **L'Homme Machine.**

Four-brained humans cannot accept a scientific neurogenetic ontology which

---

One cannot evolve from one's robothood until one realizes how totally one has been robotized.

places reality within the changing flux of the nervous system and not in the comforting solidity of the imprinted-conditioned reality-islands. "Man the machine" is an unbearable concept to those who are not ready to mutate beyond the lower, robot circuits.

One cannot evolve from one's robothood until one realizes how totally one has been robotized. A succinct presentation of this point will be found in Gurdjieff's comments on mechanization quoted by Ouspensky: In Search of the Miraculous.

Exo-psychology suggests that there are as many realities as there are neuro-anatomical structures for transceiving signals. As the seven neuro-anatomical circuits unfold, so do seven broad classes of reality.*

1. **The First Reality, Bio-cellular,** is the imprinted-conditioned world of the infant perpetuated in the viscerotonic survival techniques of the adult.

2. **The Second Reality, Locomotor-muscular,** is the imprinted-conditioned world of the crawling, brawling, walking child perpetuated in the emotional-political techniques of the adult.

3. **The Third Reality,** mediated by the left cortex, is the imprinted-conditioned world of the child learning to manipulate L.M. symbols and perpetuated in the linguistic-technology of the adult.

4. **The Fourth Reality** is the imprinted-conditioned world of social-sexual, domestic responsibility.

5. **The Fifth Reality, Body Consciousness** is the reception by the body of direct, natural signals uncensored by survival imprints and selectively aware of the demands of gravity.

6. **The Sixth Reality** is the imprint of the nervous system of and by and unto itself. Einsteinian consciousness no longer frozen to larval circuits or to the body. Brain reality is a relativistic, changing Niagara of millions of bio-electric signals flashing around a thirty-billion cell network. The statement "consciousness is no longer frozen" is not metaphorical; it refers to biochemical-electrical changes at the synaptic level which liberate the flow of signals from routine patterns. The term "static, imprinted-conditioned world" refers to neural-wired programs hooked to reality-islands.

7. **The Seventh Reality** is the reception by the nervous system of RNA signals from DNA molecules within the cell. Genetic messages leading to symbiotic inter-species telepathy. Since reality is energy registered by neural structure, we can "see" only what we are ready instrumentally and conceptually to receive. At the Seventh Circuit DNA-RNA signals are monitored.

*The **Eighth Reality** is meta-physiological, meta-biological and involves contelligence projected out from the Quantum Projection Booth. See the publications of the Physics-Consciousness Research Group by Sarfatti, Sirag, Herbert et al.

S. M. I^2. L. E.
Space Migration
Intelligence Increase
Life Extension

Exo-psychology defines an Interstellar Neurogenetic outlining the DNA pre-programmed course of individual and species evolution.

A complete philosophic system generally includes:

1. A cosmological explanation about where we came from and how it got started

2. A political theory explaining the factors involved in the destructive and harmonious expressions of territorial autonomy, control, freedom, restraint, mobility

3. An epistemological theory defining truth-falsity and right-wrong

4. An ethic defining good-bad, virtue-sin

5. An aesthetic defining beautiful-ugly, artistic-unartistic

6. An ontology defining the spectrum of realities

7. A genetic teleology explaining where biological evolution is going and how it will all turn out, and

8. An ultimate metaphysiological neuro-atomic eschatology explaining what happens when consciousness leaves the body.

The aim of Life is:

S.M.I^2.L.E.

Space Migration

Intelligence Increase

Life Extension

We are designed to Use our Heads (I^2) in order to Use Time (L.E.) in order to Use Space (S.M.).

Of these three associated imperatives Intelligence Increase is the most important. When the human has learned how to use the brain as instrument to:

4. selectively re-imprint the four terrestrial circuits

5. control the body

6. master the creation of multiple realities by means of serial re-imprinting

7. imprint (i.e. experientially identify with the DNA code)

8. decipher nuclear-quantum intelligence

then Life Extension and Space Migration will be attained.

The egocentricity and geo-centricity of larval philosophy has over-estimated human intelligence in relationship to other forms— in particular the DNA code and the atomic nucleus.

The ultimate question is: what is the end point of biological evolution?

The exo-psychological answer: contelligence mutates by fusing with, being absorbed by metaphysiological structures found in nuclear-quantum-gravitational force fields.

Neurologically it could be said that the emergence of each new neural circuit involves a "death-rebirth." The Neonate infant molts and becomes the mobile child. Although the "reality" of the infant is surely different from that of the "same" individual at age 18, the first brain remains linked to, part of the evolving neural network. Thus, in the evolution of the individual, the emergence of new neural circuits defines a series of incorporative re-incarnations. Metamorphoses.*

Genetics defines another, more enduring form of perpetuation. The DNA code is designed to keep itself alive, to remain immortal. If, as exo-psychology suggests, we can imprint DNA, learn how to consciously decipher RNA signals, we can experience the DNA time blueprint which contains the program of neural evolution back three billion years and forward for several billion years. The DNA registers and remembers signals received by the body and the nervous system which it currently "drives." Each of us thus lives on via absorption in DNA.

But neurological and genetic re-incarnation processes are still biological. Contelligence at the level of nerve cells and protein molecules obviously cannot compare with the scope, speed and power of elemental sub-nuclear processes.

The egocentricity and geo-centricity of larval philosophy has over-estimated human intelligence in relationship to other energy forms—in particular the DNA code and the atomic nucleus. Larval science would have us believe that the universe is made up of chemical elements and atomic particles which operate in blind passivity to physical laws; that at a certain point in the history of planet earth certain molecules were accidentally induced by means of lightning bolts to form the protein-nucleotides which, through chance, began to replicate; and that through a process of random selection and mutation the biological forms evolved. The summit of this blind evolutionary process, we are told, is homo-sapiens. "Man" is believed to be the only self-conscious, intelligent form on the planet and probably in the universe!

Exo-psychology suggests that this flattering self-appraisal is false—an error which leads both the arrogance and the frightened pessimism which characterize human philosophy.

From the exo-psychological point of view all biological forms are transient robots created by DNA to house and transport the genetic "brain," DNA. Just as the Third-Circuit L.M. muscular mind designs and constructs machines to serve human

---

*Exo-psychology predicts that, in the development of the individual child the activation of each unfolding circuit is preceded by a pre-molt crisis. Psychologists and educated parents in the future will learn how to anticipate, recognize the emergence of pre-molt crises and to guide the child through the unsettling phases.

The genetic code is surely not an accidental adhesion of molecules. It is an instrumental message, an energy directive created by a meta-biological intelligence.

purpose, so has DNA built fragile, replicable organisms, including humans. It is apparently difficult for the human mind to conceive of the degree to which DNA intelligence is superior to the human intellect. The complexities and time spans dealt with by DNA are as superior to human intelligence as the human is to a wind-up doll.

The great primitive exo-psychologist William Blake posed the question:

"Tyger, tyger, burning bright,

In the forests of the night,

What immortal hand or eye

Dare frame thy fearful symmetry?"

The answer is DNA.

And what enduring intelligence burning bright in the forests of the night-time sky designed DNA?

The genetic code is surely not an accidental adhesion of molecules. It is an instrumental message, an energy directive created by a meta-biological intelligence.

This intelligence is astrophysical and galactic in scope, pervasive, ubiquitous, but miniaturized in quanta structure. Just as the multi-billion year blue-print of biological evolution is packaged within the nucleus of every cell, so may the quantum-mechanical blueprint of astronomical evolution be found in the nucleus of the atom.

We have defined consciousness as energy received by structure. And we have defined intelligence as energy transmitted by structure. The contelligence of life-forms is shaped and limited by anatomy and organic form. Sub-atomic-gravitational force fields are obviously capable of faster, more complex and more extensive levels of consciousness and intelligence.

Exo-psychology hypothesizes that the evolution of astro-physical structures involves a contelligence as superior to DNA as DNA is to neuron-brains.

The direction of organic evolution now can be stated. Starting with unicell organisms, life produces a series of neural circuits and increasingly more complex-and-efficient bodies to transport and facilitate higher contelligence. The culmination of this biological process is the seven-circuit brain which is able to communicate with DNA, i.e. receive, integrate and transmit information at the level of RNA.

Among the byproducts of the seven-circuit brain contelligence are telepathy and inter-species symbiosis (including symbiosis with the more advanced species which probably exist on half of the millions of inhabited planets in our local galaxy).*

---

*Telepathy (i.e. neuro-electric communication) is a post-terrestrial phenomenon. Telepathic communication cannot occur while we are crawling around on the bottom of a 4000 mile atmosphere ocean any more than vocal-symbolic communication can occur among marine animals. We have to crawl out of the water to activate the Third-circuit (left brain). When we leave the surface of the planet and live in free space, telepathy (Sixth circuit contelligence) will occur.

. . .if we can figure out the possible nature of a Higher quantum-mechanical Contelligence, certainly "they" who await in the genetic future can do as well or better.

The eighth phase of evolution is transformation of contelligence to meta-physiological, neuro-atomic structures. This quantum-mechanical process does not necessarily involve the destruction of organic memories or biological contelligence— but probably an incorporation of the neurogenetic into the nuclear-gravitational-quantum.

Metaphysiological contelligence transceives at the speed and frequency of nuclear particles and can create matter, i.e. arrange atoms in architected patterns. Such a level of contelligence could construct pre-programmed DNA codes as simply as humans now build computer-directed manufacturing processes.

It is, of course, almost impossible for the primitive L.M. symbolic mind to conceive of the capacities of quantum intelligence. Does not logic, however, force us to accept the probability of this Higher Form of contelligence? The only other cosmological-eschatological alternatives currently offered are:

- accidental, haphazard clustering of proteins and carbohydrates triggered by lightning bolts in the Pre-Cambrian slime leaving "man" the highest dismal form of a ruthless survival battle, or
- anthropomorphized police-court Jehovahs of monotheism.

The very fact that some primitive human beings can conceive of superior meta-physiological contelligence specifically based upon current scientific evidence encourages us to assume that Higher Contelligence can at least equal our extrapolations and empirically-based speculations. To put it bluntly, if we can figure out the possible nature of a higher quantum-mechanical Contelligence, certainly "they" who await in the genetic future can do as well or better.*

To summarize this summary of the 8th Eschatological Circuit: organic life evolves to become part of a metaphysiological contelligence which is nuclear-gravitational in structure, and which creates unified force-fields, galactic in scope, quantum in nature.

---

*Who are they? They are we-in-the-future.

Just as the members of insect colonies are genetically pre-programmed to play certain roles necessary for hive survival—worker, drone, warrior, fertile male, brood queen—so are there twelve larval types of human.

Larval realities are defined by islands of local environment attached to the nervous system at the time of imprinting.

From the scientific viewpoint reality is an ocean of electromagnetic vibrations whirling constantly through different cycles of speed and swirling momentarily into temporary structures including bodies with nervous systems.

The human nervous system is genetically designed to receive a small band of waves along the cyclic frequency spectrum.

Human consciousness, i.e personal reality, is determined by the point along the frequency spectrum where the neural dials are tuned.

In a previous section it was suggested that the nervous system has evolved through twelve larval-terrestrial stages and will in the future metamorphize through twelve post-terrestrial stages. As new species emerged, new and more complex stages of the nervous system evolved. Uni-cellular species remain at the primitive level of approach-avoidance. Most mammalian forms remain at the level of individual muscular dominance. Others, the herd-flock species, reach a level of pre-symbolic social communication. Primitive humanoids remain at a level of symbol-manipulation and artifact construction but do not attain domestication and the division of sexual responsibility manifested by homo sapiens and some insects.

In companion books **The Periodic Table of Evolution** and **The Game of Life**, it is hypothesized that systematic seasonal variations in solar radiation create alterations in DNA templating at the time of conception which determine human neurogenetic "types." And that the twelve Zodiac "signs" may crudely personalize twelve species very different in neurological wiring which reflect and recapitulate twelve stages of phylogenetic and human evolution. Each Zodiac "species" thus represents the mastery of one of the twelve neurological stages which are involved in the evolution of life on our planet—preparatory for extra-terrestrial migration.*

Just as the members of insect colonies are genetically pre-programmed to play certain roles necessary for hive survival—worker, drone, warrior, fertile male, brood queen—so are there twelve larval types of human.

These genetic types have been vulgarly popularized as the twelve Zodiac signs, the first twelve Tarot personages, the twelve Greco-Roman divinities. Each of these twelve types can be considered as genetically separate; each contributes to the human larval evolutionary process and each carries a printed-out nervous system geared to a specialized survival task.

In addition to genetic specializations, the environmental models imprinted at the four periods of individual development define island realities which vary from person-

*The tradition of using twelve peers in a trial by jury may be an unconscious recognition of the twelve species of humans which populate larval society.

Anyone who is different is crazy or alien. Xenophobia is based on primate neurology. The hive cannot tolerate their realities.

to-person and from group-to-group. The language and dialects to which the child is exposed during the emergence of the Third Circuit lay down muscular patterns in the larynx and hand which are fixed and which limit the cognitive-symbolic reality.

This unique specificity of reality means, among other things, that we find twelve larval species and numerous cultural-imprint groups of human beings wandering around the planet, for the most part existing in different realities. To add to the confusion, since the 1960's we have several million half-mutated Hippies floating aimlessly.

People unconsciously recognize this selectivity of island realities. Social avoidance and clustering tend to respond to these reality chauvinisms. Anyone who is different is crazy or alien. Xenophobia is based on primate neurology. The hive cannot tolerate other realities.

Ontological chauvinisms are deeply rooted in fixed genetic and neural structures. In spite of the ignorance about their neural machinery, human robots manage to communicate with each other about material needs with amazing efficiency.

The imprint is a neuro-umbilical life-line extended from the nervous system to that energy cluster on the planetary surface that offers material, survival stimuli.

The discovery of neural imprinting could be one of the four most important intellectual achievements of the human race. The other three are: the Einsteinian-quantum-mechanical equations involving space-time-energy; the astronomical location of earth in the highly populated galaxy; and the decoding of the genetic-evolutionary process which makes possible bio-chemical longevity, genetic control and symbiotic communication.

Understanding of the sequential imprinting of the nervous system adds the fourth card to the Psi-Phy deck.

Imprinting is the process by which neural circuits mediating specific neuro-umbilical survival behaviors (along paths of discharge laid out in advance) select the stimulus in the environment, internal or external, which determines the timing and direction and object of the discharge.

The imprint is a neuro-umbilical life-line extended from the nervous system to that energy cluster on the planetary surface that offers· material, survival stimuli. Once attached, the larval nervous system is hooked for life—unless retracted by accidental trauma; or retracted deliberately—in which case post-larval contelligence is attained.

The facts about imprinting originally came from the science of ethology, "the comparative study of animal behavior under natural conditions or of laboratory study which utilizes methods and problems suggested by field observations," (William Etkin).

Konrad Lorentz and Nico Tinbergen were recently (1973) awarded the Nobel Prize for their pioneering work in this field.

The most fascinating aspect of the imprinting process is this; the original selection of the external stimulus which triggers off the pre-designed response does not derive from a normal learning process but a short exposure during a brief, specific "critical period" of the animal's life.

The infant body is like a space ship floating on the strange new planet. The imprint is a life-line extended in blind robot fashion groping for hospitable surface to which it attaches and roots—thus creating the reality island.

"If imprinting is not accomplished during the first few days of existence, it will not "take" at any other time. Such an animal will fail to respond appropriately to any other animal, and no amount of association with members of its species will bring out the response." (Etkin.)

It has been found that "if young birds are handled by the experimenter during their first few hours of life, they will thereafter react to him and to other human beings as they normally would to their parents." The groping neuro-umbilical attaches to the first warm, moving body it contacts.

"Most remarkable, indeed, is the fact that when the animal which has been imprinted to a human being becomes mature many months later, it will show courting

The infant body is like a space ship floating on the strange new planet. The imprint is a life-line extended in blind robot fashion groping for hospitable surface to which it attaches and roots— thus creating the reality island.

responses to humans even in preference to its own species. Hand-trained birds commonly display courting behaviors to the trainer's hands."

The implications of imprinting theory applied to human behavior are embarrassing to our rational conceptions of self, ego, conscious choice; indeed, they suggest an ontological helplessness which takes on the dimensions of a Sci-Fi robot tale. The neurological situation is as follows: The human body is made up of many receiving organs and discharge systems which are controlled by the nervous system, a communication network of some thirty billion cells. Each organ of the body is wired by a complex pattern of nerve fibres. Each neuron receives, evaluates and transmits information to as many as 60,000 other neurons. The particular wiring pattern which triggers off each organ and action system of the body is programmed by imprinted stimuli. The specific stimulus which activates each neuro-umbilical survival system is determined by accidental coincidence—the external factors present during the "sensitive period." Human Beings are robots programmed and directed by neural imprints which trigger off standardized discharge patterns in response to accidentally imprinted cues.

The newborn baby is equipped with the behavior patterns necessary for immediate survival: to turn towards the mothering stimulus and suckle. Shortly after birth the baby's nervous system takes a picture, i.e. focuses all the sensory equipment on the soft, warm, milk-producing stimulus and permanently photographs this picture as "survivally good" and safe. If this viscerotonic imprint is not taken because of absence during the critical period of the appropriate stimulus, the basic "survival security" system is not effectively wired-up to human contacts.*

A most crucial aspect of neural imprinting is that the four larval neural circuits unfold chronologically. Each of the four neuro-umbilical life-lines is extended in turn when each neural circuit emerges.

For example, before adolescence the sexual circuit is rudimentary. During adolescence dramatic physiological and anatomical changes occur in the primary and secondary sexual organs. These changes are so pronounced that we might with wisdom speak of a metamorphosis analogous to the transformation of the insect from larva to butterfly. At this time the neural circuit which mediates sexual activity unfolds. There is a critical or "sensitive" period of sexual imprinting. The sexual antennae emerge and blindly scan for a place to root.

The first time the sexual system is fired in all-out response, a sexual imprint is taken. The state of activity of the entire neural system at the time of imprint determines the way the sexual system is wired—i.e. the cues which arouse it. The sensory, emotional, mental and social stimuli form a pattern (sexual climate) which facilitates

*Failure on the part of the neonate to imprint a human target for the First Circuit creates childhood schizophrenia, the autistic child. This process and its remedy are discussed in sections 1.3, 1.4, and 1.5 of the book The Eight Calibre Brain.

The accidental vicissitudes of Fourth Circuit sexual imprinting have been well known to psychiatrists. Early erections and orgasms can create kinky fetishes.

subsequent arousal and discharge.

The accidental vicissitudes of Fourth Circuit sexual imprinting have been well known to psychiatrists. Early erections and orgasms can create kinky fetishes.

The mechanics and neurologic of the mental-symbolic Third Circuit imprint are less familiar. The acquisition of speech and manipulative behavior involves a special imprinting of third brain wiring of laryngeal and manual muscles. Thinking is accomplished by moving the nine muscles of the larynx. During the period when the child is mastering speech, the mental style of the contiguous human models is being absorbed. These models are parents, and, more important, older children. The tender tendrils of symbolic mental activity are extended. This is a most vulnerable period. The mental styles and emotional models of the people in the environment determine whether the child's mind is open, trusting, or withdrawn, rejecting.

The child imprints (wires up) a specific method of thinking. Once this intellectual pattern is imprinted, subsequent education has little effect on the modes of mental manipulation. The eight cognitive modes used by the laryngeal-muscle-mind are described in Chapter 3 of The Eight Calibre Brain. The imprint attaches to the model present at the critical period of extension.

1. Circuit 1 biosurvival language is global. The movements and sounds which say, "I am safe," "you are safe," are recognized by almost all animals regardless of culture. Behaviors which express pain or physical threat are also generally recognized. We speak here of eating, vomiting, sucking, disgust, embracing, moaning, physically aggressing or menacing.

2. Circuit 2 emotional language: Gestures, postures and verbal tones which communicate a status message are almost universally recognized. The gestural signals for affiliation, dominance, submission, begging, giving, coercion and passive complaint require no cross-cultural dictionary. However each culture has a specific vocabulary of status—accents, gestures, ornaments, conspicuous possessions, postures.

At one point a Cadillac car indicates highest status; shortly later a Cadillac indicates a pimp or cocaine dealer from the slums. And so it goes.

3. Circuit 3 L.M. language: Symbols and artifacts are limited in comprehensibility to cultural groups which share the similar imprint, i.e. were exposed at the critical period to the same styles of laryngeal dexterity and manual symbolization. Class, caste, and craft-guild issues are important. Included in these Third Circuit cultures are:

> artifact groups
> verbal dialect groups
> literacy groups
> scientific groups
> occupational groups
> sports and game groups

The child imprints, wires up a specific method of thinking. Once this intellectual pattern is imprinted, subsequent education has little effect on the modes of mental manipulation.

A central concept in exo-psychology is this notion of personal neural-reality, which differs from person to person. Each of us deals with a world which is defined by a unique pattern of neural wires and fixed umbilical life-lines. Just as we can try to understand the emerging stages of human development by analogy to the metamorphosis of insects (since we are too close to the situation to appreciate metamorphosis in ourselves), so we can understand the electro-neural uniqueness of "reality" by considering the consciousness islands of other species.

Consider the snake. Observing with our optical scanners we "see" a mouse run across the floor and a snake turn its head and strike. We assume that the snake "sees" what we see: a furry, brown animal. A study of the snake's neural receptors indicates, however, that the snake uses heat receptors to locate prey. What the snake senses is a neon spot of "warm" moving across its screen. It is robot programmed to strike at "heat."

Human beings often interact across similar "reality" gulfs. They are robot-programmed as differently among the selves as the human and the snake.

Humans vary in the number of L.M. languages they can exchange. Some, the most primitive, communicate only in the oral dialect of their childhood neighborhood and can manipulate only the simple muscle-moved artifacts of village life.

The highly civilized larval has mastered hundreds of L.M. symbol systems. An educated Russian or American can speak and write each other in several languages, cooperatively manipulate a wide variety of mechanical artifacts, professional sequences, scientific codes, sports and game rituals.

In communicating with a larval, once it has been established by non-verbal cues that Circuit 1 is safe and Circuit 2 is cooperative, the next step is to establish which L.M. muscle-thought languages are shared and can be appropriately exchanged. Most larval interactions are brief and limited. Artifact transactions. Buying. Selling. Service performances. Superficial socializing designed to elicit cultural reassurance. Extended L.M. symbol conversations are loaded with complexity because emotional factors inevitably intrude. The giving of information to others is often resented because the possession of information implies power.

The Third Circuit of the nervous system is activated when the young child is in a position of weakness. Those who teach the L.M. symbol systems are adults or superiors. The ability to learn symbols is determined by the emotional context—the person with the information is placed in a superior position over the receiver.

The nervous system is interconnected by means of synaptic links. The synapse is the gap between two neurons across which the nerve impulse flows. The synaptic connection is chemical. Just as chemicals "fix" the photographic image on film, so is the neural image of the island-reality "fixed" by synaptic chemical bonds at the time of imprinting.

The robot truth is this: the patterns of neural connection create the picture of reality.

We believe that we are imprinted to believe. We think that the tiny turf to which our neuro-umbilical life-lines attach is "reality."

The human nervous system imprints social cues. A child growing up finds a certain stability and consistency in the social cues SHe imprints. Hir parents speak the same language, share rituals with the family next door. This consensual agreement provides the illusion of a "reality" shared with those in Hir culture group. "Sanity" is defined in terms of one's ability to convince oneself that SHe perceives what others do. Festinger and other social psychologists have conducted "cognitive dissonance" experiments which show how easily and naturally human beings distort objective data to fit neural expectations.

Social consciousness is a web of neuro-umbilical fabrication woven by conditioning and continual adaptive distortion.

We believe what we are imprinted to believe. We think that the tiny turf to which our neuro-umbilical life-lines attach is "reality."

The fact of separate, subjective realities based on individual imprints (reality islands) is frightening for the pre-neurological human to accept. We recall the parable of the eight blind men and the elephant. This separateness accounts for the terror that is felt in the presence of an "insane" person. In many cases the person called "insane" or "hallucinating" is actually aware of the neural insulation which separates people and might be considered more sane and accurate than the deluded "normals." Ontological terror is the naive reaction to the discovery that there are other realities beyond one's own imprint and learned neural patterns.

We have used the metaphor of neuro-umbilical life-lines to describe the attachment of the nervous system to local environments via imprint. Security means that the imprinted life-lines are securely fastened to a stable island-reality.

Another metaphor often used by neurologicians to describe the creation and limitation of subjective reality by imprint is the "bubble." Castaneda's don Juan gives a good description of the reality-of-the-imprint which he calls tonal.

"Sorcerers say that we are inside a bubble. It is a bubble into which we are placed at the moment of our birth. At first the bubble is open, but then it begins to close until it has sealed us in. That bubble is our perception.*

We live inside that bubble all of our lives. And what we witness on its round walls is our own reflection. . .The thing reflected is our own view of the world. That view is first a description, which is given to us at the moment of our birth [more accurately, the moment of imprint] until all our attention is caught by it and the description becomes a view," [that is to say, a reality].

from Tales of Power, pp. 246-247

---

*Don Juan consistently uses the word "perception" to describe consciousness. The formation of the "imprint-bubble" can be clearly "seen," experienced during L.S.D. sessions.

The only way to rewire neural patterns is to interfere with the neurotransmitter sequence at the synapse, thus retracting the old imprint and allowing for a new imprinting.

Let us, for a moment, visualize the nervous system by itself (apart from the body) as a bio-computer with 30 billion reception-evaluation-output centers (neurons) wired-up together and mediated by hierarchical centers. The various sense organs receive billions of signals a minute. The output fibres fire billions of signals per minute. Imprints lay down the basic connections which pattern and guide neural activity.

There is, for example, the First Circuit emergency system which, when the "danger" cues are received and evaluated, commands millions of survival actions. Early "danger" imprints and genetic programs cue this powerful, basic system which effects, when mobilized, every organ in the body. Fear! Once the First Circuit has imprinted a fear stimulus, the only way this chemico-electric synaptic pattern can be changed is to suspend or replace the wiring. The intransigence of human "phobias" and "security-blankets" is caused by imprints.

The only way to rewire neural patterns is to interfere with the neurotransmitter sequence at the synapse, thus retracting the old imprint and allowing for a new imprinting. Shock, illness, trauma, drugs, child delivery, stimulus deprivation and electrical charge are the only ways to change the chemistry of the synapse. When action inside the body becomes overwhelmingly intense so as to alter synapse chemistry, the imprint life-lines to the external environment are retracted. The chance to re-imprint is offered.

When the concept of neural imprinting is understood, techniques for psychological treatment will be changed. The doctor will teach the patient the principles of re-imprinting and the patient will select the new reality SHe wishes to create. Democracy and collaboration are necessary in neurologic treatment. The doctor cannot prescribe or control the treatment, because the result is a new reality for the patient.

Medical practice will also be altered. Infection or malfunction of an organ of the body can produce chemical changes which require recircuiting the neural wiring. When the somatic infection is cured the emergency "sick" wiring may remain in operation preventing the restoration of normal function. Conversely, infection or malfunction may require curative changes which are blocked by the normal "wiring." This view of the nervous system as a programmed bio-electrical network may help explain the "mysteries" of acupuncture. The needles have little effect on the fleshly system, but, particularly when energized with mild electric charges, may affect the synaptic programs which regulate the function of the organ. In the near future we may see Neurologic replace psychology and Neurosomatic-medicine replace the vague concept of psychosomatic medicine.

To understand the learning process it is necessary to understand the primary role of the imprint and the secondary role of the conditioned-association.

The notion of imprinting has created some confusion in psychology because it suggests a form of "learning" which is immediate and irreversible, quite in contrast to conditioned learning which is the foundation of most psychological theories. According to the classic definition: "Learning is a relatively permanent change in behavior that occurs as the result of practice." Learning is based on associating one stimulus or response with another on the basis of reward or punishment. Psychological theories of learning are based upon observations of external visible behavior and pay little attention to the internal, invisible neurological situation.

The classic studies of conditioning were executed by Ivan Pavlov, the Russian physiologist.

> 'While studying the relatively automatic reflexes associated with digestion, Pavlov noticed that the flow of saliva to food placed in the mouth of the dog was influenced not only by the food placed in the dog's mouth but also by the sight of food. He interpreted the flow of saliva to food placed in the mouth as an unlearned response, as he called it, an **unconditioned** response. But surely, he thought, the influence of the sight of food has to be learned. Hence this is a learned or conditioned response.' — Hilgard and Atkinson, Introduction to **Psychology**, Harcourt Brace.
>
> Later research demonstrated that animals could be conditioned to salivate in response to a flashing light, sounds, visual forms, etc. 'The conditioned response may be considered a simple habit because 1) an association is demonstrated to exist between a stimulus and a response, and 2) this association is a learned one.'

To understand the learning process it is necessary to understand the primary role of the imprint and the secondary role of the conditioned-association. The imprint hooks the natural unconditioned response to an external stimulus—the releaser mechanism. The conditioned stimulus is associated with the imprinted stimulus. Imprinting is the basic connection between the external stimulus and the nerve endings; and between the nerve endings and the response.

Conditioning then connects (wires up neurally) other stimuli which are associated with the imprinted stimuli. The learned stimuli can then trigger off the response connected neurally to the original imprinted stimulus.

If the infant's First Circuit is positively imprinted to Mother, other stimuli associated with Mother become learned cues which can trigger off the "positive-approach" response. The infant's First Circuit is negatively imprinted to stimuli—tastes, smells, forms—which are noxious or dangerous. Stimuli associated with "danger" trigger off the withdrawal reaction (fear).

The imprint hooks the natural unconditioned response to an external stimulus—the releaser mechanism.

Conditioning psychologists have studied the relationships between unconditioned stimulus-response units and learned reactions in terms of the similarity of stimuli (generalization), the reinforcement or reward of the conditioned stimulus-response by the unconditioned, the waning or extinction of the learned association in the absence of the unconditioned reward, discrimination of differences between stimuli, etc.

Classical (Pavlovian) conditioning focuses on the presentation of conditioned stimuli in association with the original unconditioned stimulus to the response (e.g., salivation).

Skinnerism is the crowning philosophy of the Third Circuit society, the mechanical civilization which began in the neolithic and which climaxed in Henry Ford's assembly lines.

Operant conditioning studies behavior which bears little resemblance to the genetically pre-programmed behavior that is normally elicited by the reinforcing stimulus (i.e. salivation is the dog's normal response to food but rolling over is not). B. F. Skinner, the founder of the school of operant conditioning, distinguishes between respondent and operant behavior.

'Respondent behavior is directly under the control of the stimulus, as in the unconditioned reflexes of classical conditioning: the flow of saliva in the mouth, the constriction of the pupil to a flash of light on the eye, the knee jerk to a tap on the patellar tendon. The relation of operant behavior to stimulation is somewhat different. The behavior often appears to be emitted; that is, it appears to be spontaneous rather than a response to stimulation. . .When operant behavior becomes related to a stimulus (as when I answer the ringing telephone), the ringing telephone is a discriminated stimulus, telling me that the telephone is answerable, but it does not force me to answer. Even though the ringing telephone is compelling, the response to it is operant and not respondent behavior.

'The word operant derives from the fact that operant behavior "operates" on the environment to produce some effect. Thus going to where the telephone is and raising the receiver from the hook are operant acts that lead to the telephone conversation.

'To produce operant conditioning in the laboratory, a hungry rat is placed in a box. . .The inside of the box is plain, except for the protruding bar with the food dish beneath it.

'. . .the experimenter attaches the food magazine, so that every time the rat presses the bar a pellet of food falls into the dish. The rat eats and soon presses the bar again. The food reinforces bar-pressing. . .

'With this illustration before us, we are ready to consider the meaning of conditioned operant behavior. As indicated above, it "operates" on the environment; the rat's bar-pressing produces or gains access to the food. In classical conditioning the animal is passive; it merely waits until the conditioned stimulus is presented and is followed by the unconditioned stimulus. In operant conditioning the animal has to be active; its behavior cannot be reinforced unless it does something.

'A large part of human behavior may be classified as operant— turning a key in a lock, driving a car, writing a letter, carrying on a conversation. Such activities are not elicited by an unconditioned stimulus of the Pavlovian type. But once the behavior occurs it can be reinforced according to the principles of operant conditioning.'

Skinnerism is the final philosophic statement of the puritanical protestant-ethic manipulators who dominated the world for 400 years up to Hiroshima.

> '. . .[operant] behavior is sometimes called instrumental behavior because it produces effects just as a tool or other instrument does. Hence operant conditioning is also known as instrumental conditioning.' — Hilgard and Atkinson, ibid.

We have considered these definitions and principles because operant conditioning and behavior modification are becoming popular and politically potent aspects of the current behavior-control movement. An increasing number of psychologists are employing conditioning techniques to "shape" the behavior of people who are judged to be disturbed or anti-social; these in addition to the legions of psychologists who attempt to manipulate the behaviors of others in advertising, education and mass media propaganda.

Neurologic may help people to understand what conditioning psychologists are trying to do and why they are doomed to failure.

Conditioning psychologists are behaviorists. They are concerned with observable, measurable movements in space-time. Behaviorism developed in the 1920's as a reaction to "introspective," "faculty" psychology which explained human nature in terms of invisible emotional and mental states attributed to the conscious "mind." Behaviorism, unhappily, chose to model itself after Newtonian mechanistic visible physics just at the point when Einsteinian concepts and invisible states were emerging. In the last half century we have seen an increasing "interiorization" of physics and genetics. The significant (and significantly overlooked) fact about the new micro-sciences is that functions, meanings, lawful regularities have been located in internal structures invisible to the naked eye which are, in many cases, similar to the spiritual faculties assigned by psychoanalysts, theologians and philosophers to metaphysical entities within the human "soul" or "psyche." Ancient Hindu theories about the unity of consciousness, for example, now find empirical confirmation in descriptions of the nervous system as an interconnected network of thirty billion cells. Ancient Vedic concepts of the unity of life are confirmed by the discovery that there is only a slight difference in the amino acid configuration which makes up the genetic material of all living entities, plants and primates. The theories of physicists like Jack Sarfatti and John Archibald Wheeler bring consciousness back to the center of the nuclear and quantum-mechanical stage.

When we review the work of conditioning psychologists from the perspective of a seven-circuit (plus one) nervous system, we can see precisely where and why behaviorism is limited. Operant conditioning is concerned with the behavior mediated by the social brain. Learned instrumental actions. Skinnerism is the crowning philosophy of the Third Circuit society, the mechanical civilization which began in the neolithic and which climaxed in Henry Ford's assembly lines. Skinnerism is the final philosophic statement of the puritanical protestant-ethic manipulators who dominated the world for 400 years up to Hiroshima. In this context let us reconsider the ominous surgical

The significant (and significantly overlooked) fact about the new micro-sciences is that functions, meanings, lawful regularities have been located in internal structures invisible to the naked eye which are, in many cases, similar to the spiritual faculties assigned by psychoanalysts, theologians and philosophers to metaphysical entities within the human "soul" or "psyche."

implications of the standard definition: "The word operant derives from the fact that operant behavior 'operates' on the environment to produce some effect. . .To produce operant conditioning. . .a hungry rat is placed in a box. . .A large part of human behavior may be classified as operant—turning a key in a lock, driving a car. . ." This is the third brain at work.

During World War II Professor Skinner was in charge of a War Department Project to train pigeons to peck at panels which would home unmanned bombers into "enemy" targets.

There is another aspect of the operant conditioning model which merits comment.

Humanity has evolved to the point where the knowledge of how to control the nervous system is available. Neurologic has developed rudimentary methods for suspending imprints and creating new neural imprints. Although this knowledge is uneasily suppressed, the basic concept that "reality" is created by the individual nervous system is understood by millions of persons born after 1945.

Skinnerians attempt to "shape" Third Circuit symbolic, manipulative behavior. This can be a futile or dangerously coercive business. Operant conditioning "works" by means of immediate and continual reinforcement. Imprinting requires no reinforcement. As the Psi-Phy Jesuit might say: let me imprint the infant and you can futilely try to condition the child; let me imprint the child and you can futilely try to condition the adolescent; let me imprint the adolescent and you can futilely try to condition the adult.

The imprint requires no repeated reward or punishment. The neural fix is permanent. Only bio-chemical shock can loosen the neuro-umbilical lines. The conditioned association, on the contrary, wanes and disappears with lack of repetition.

And neural imprints are themselves derivative structures compared with genetic templates which determine the form of the neural robot.

Neural imprints are accidental, local targets for the bio-electric forcefields laid down by DNA, which organize RNA to construct the body and the nervous system.

Humanity has evolved to the point where the knowledge of how to control the nervous system is available. Neurologic has developed rudimentary methods for suspending imprints and creating new neural imprints. Although this knowledge is uneasily suppressed, the basic concept that "reality" is created by the individual nervous system is understood by millions of persons born after 1945.

But genetic engineering is much more important than neural engineering. The research of Paul, Stein and Kleinsmith on non-histone proteins which turn-on DNA offer the key to genetic control. And the work of Bruce Niklas at Duke reminds us of the intransigence of chromosomal patterns which determine body structure.*

There are two groups of technocrats clamoring to change the behavior of their fellow citizens. Right-wing punitive coercers. And liberal rewarders. The attempts of both groups of bureaucrats are futile because they attempt to re-condition—rather than re-imprint.

Punitive coercion works only as long as the threat remains and thus requires a police state.

The liberal social psychologists believe that they can change behavior by democratic, supportive, egalitarian education methods. Head-start programs. Peace Corps.

---

*Niklas reports that if chromosome strands are experimentally disarrayed (by poking them with a micro-needle) the molecules move back into the original sequence—much the way iron filings "swim" into position in response to magnetism. This suggests that some sort of energy-field pattern operates to keep the DNA code coherent and logical. A microscopic genetic brain integrates and controls the evolutionary signal.

Chapter 20

Symbol-stupidity is so pervasive in every larval society that there is almost no chance for a child to be exposed to an open, fast, mobile, factually truthful, electrically circuited mind.

Behavior-modification. Bussing. Tutoring. Scholarship payments. Insight therapies. Mental health methods.

These liberal approaches fail to effect change and serve only to support the "humanist" welfare bureaucracy.

The experimental psychologists, for whom B. F. Skinner is spokesman, are more intelligent. They believe that they can impose behavior change by means of involuntary operant conditioning. This, however, requires total and continual control of reinforcements—rewards and punishments. The problem is that psychological methods work only when the conditioners are continually present to reinforce. The liberals have to be there constantly doling out welfare payments, scholarships, grants, interpersonal strokes.

The Skinnerian manipulators must be there constantly controlling environmental response.

As soon as the "subjects" are left alone to their own devices they immediately drift back to the magnetism of the imprint (and the structure of the genetic template).

This creates no problem with domesticated middle-class people who have imprinted the docility and fear which provide internal controls for the Second Circuit, the repetitious symbol manipulation of the Third Circuit and the "shame" of the Fourth Circuit. Society's schools carefully imprint children to be stupid so that it is a simple, rote matter to inhibit questioning intelligence. Symbol-stupidity is so pervasive in every larval society that there is almost no chance for a child to be exposed to an open, fast, mobile, factually truthful, electrically circuited mind. The inefficiency of psychological conditioning and the immovable solidity of imprints is seen most clearly in the Fourth Circuit. It is almost impossible to recondition a sexual imprint, to "cure" a homosexual with social-symbolic rewards or by physical punishment, electric shocks and aversion drugs. Let us inquire of the psychological conditioners how much success they have had in removing sexual fetishes, specialized imprinted lusts. When the Fourth Circuit sexual machinery is wired to a particular external lust stimulus even menopause cannot alter what biochemistry has etched, engraved, stamped-in to the synaptic linkage.

In order to condition human behavior it is necessary to get control of stimulus early in childhood and to maintain this control throughout life.

The larval societies now controlling the planet can only maintain themselves by the increasing use of coercive and manipulative conditioning methods to shape, direct and control behavior.

B. F. Skinner, the Harvard behaviorist, in his book **Beyond Freedom and Dignity**, has presented the case for the Political Conditioners. It can be paraphrased simply: "Since human beings, allowed to behave freely, will not act responsibly, they must be psychologically coerced, conditioned to be dutiful, virtuous, reliable, prompt, efficient, happy, law-abiding. Humans must be continually manipulated by rewards and punishments to do the right thing."

There are two aspects of this social conditioning regime which are not stressed by Skinner. To make it work, the government psychologists must have total control over the citizenry and there must be total secrecy and censorship.

In 1961 there came to the Center for Personality Research at Harvard University an enthusiastic Skinnerian who reported on the applications of operant conditioning to patients in a mental hospital. One of the behaviors to be inhibited was hallucinatory talk. Now there are many among us who believe that hallucinations have a functional role in the psyche and would consider the automatic extinguishing of hallucinations a violent restriction of some message that has importance in the emitter reality, even if it is not understood or considered useful to the psychologist's reality. Using the technique of immediate reinforcement, the Skinnerians would instantly produce a cigarette every time the patient made a non-hallucinatory comment and would take the cigarette away every time the patient would hallucinate. The researcher gleefully announced that the rate of hallucinatory comments dropped by a significant level. Even more impressive changes in behavior accompanied the giving or deprivation of food. The Skinnerian glumly complained that hospital rules prevented them from carrying out this experiment to the useful point of starvation. "If we had total control over food intake, we could really shape behavior," said the operant conditioner, who may or may not have heard the soft comment by one staff member that this technique had been used by most of the dictators in world history.

In order to condition human behavior it is necessary to get control of stimulus early in childhood and to maintain this control throughout life. In the psychological utopia, conditioning would be accompanied by continual psychological testing so that special aptitudes and potential trouble-makers are identified early in the game and special conditioning programs set up, tailored to eliminate individual eccentricity.

Political conditioning requires not only control of reward and punishment, but also secrecy.

One dissident, freedom-oriented psychologist can totally disrupt a psychological fascism by public exposure. If parents and even children are warned about the method of conditioning they can consciously decide whether to cooperate or to resist, passively or actively. Psychological tests are, for the most part, ineffective, if the subject has

Consider the dog who rolls over to get his bone. Will the dog roll over in the absence of the master? This is the nightmare that haunts the aging Mao.

been warned about the purpose and construction of the tests. Even the use of drugs in brainwashing can be counteracted by the person who learns about the specific effects of neuro-chemicals.

Psychological conditioning techniques cannot be employed in a democracy where minority groups can campaign against and publicly discuss the techniques being used, and publish the answers to screening tests, where citizens have the right to avoid the conditioners.

Thus the proposals of B. F. Skinner cannot be implemented except in a state where the government has total control of communication.

Without these controls continually reinforcing, continually reminding (e.g., the omnipresent slogans of the police state, the omnipresent advertising directives of the consumer state), people just plain forget what they are trained to do and drift back to their imprints. And to their genetic-robot styles.

Consider the dog who rolls over to get his bone. Will the dog roll over in the absence of the master? This is the nightmare that haunts the aging Mao.

Human behavior is determined by:

genetic-neural template (zodiac type)

and

imprint.

When the child gets to school it is too late to teach Hir. If SHe has imprinted, from hir home or peer-group, a dexterous symbolic mind, SHe will learn in spite of the teachers.*

A very thin veneer of operant-conditioned behavior creates the flimsy facade of domesticated civilization.

Larval humanity now faces a genetic cross-roads. Some will choose to solidify social conditioning by manipulating the child's environment and thus domesticating the imprint. Maoism.

Others will choose to mutate to a higher level where each person is taught to manage and control Hir own imprinting and conditioning. We can expect that many different social groups will emerge along both of these directions.

We have just considered the genetic, neural and social limitations of conditioning. We shall now consider the liberating and limiting implications of serial re-imprinting.

---

*The word "mind" refers to the basic orientation of the muscles of the larynx and the right-hand which determine the style of symbol manipulation—upon which social conditioning grafts its rewards and punishments.

The robot, operant-conditioned to symbols, is a reward addict. If we remove the symbol-rewarding environment, if we fail to produce the conditioned stimulus, the humanoid robot goes mad, because SHe has nothing to do.

Learning, conditioning and other educational or coercive methods of behavior-control write their messages on sand. After each daily tide of association and reward-punishment the associations must be repeated. The coercive nature of learned behavior is not clearly seen because it appears voluntary, indeed, the conditioned robot is obsessively drawn back to his place in the sand box. Larval civilization is a Beckett landscape. Every morning millions of humanoids rush to their sand-piles and re-construct them.

The ordeal of Sisyphus was an exciting heroic adventure compared to the monotony of social conditioning. The robot, operant-conditioned to symbols, is a reward addict. If we remove the symbol-rewarding environment, if we fail to produce the conditioned stimulus, the humanoid robot goes mad, because SHe has nothing to do. We can accurately speak of stimulus junkies. If there is no sand box and no sand to work on, there is panic. Social deprivation creates desperate reward hunger. The social reality of conditioned response requires continual rewarding. The prisoners continually rebuild their restricting reality walls which crumble if they are not continually reinforced.

Operant conditioning is robotry and can exist only in a controlled, scheduled, coercive society.

If, to continue this rather gritty metaphor, conditioning is building sand structures, imprinting is like stamped-out metal patterns. Trying to recondition an imprint with reward-punishment is like dropping single grains of sand on a forged steel pattern. Decades of sand can wear away the iron pattern. Senility can wear down the imprint. The aging politician gets lazy, the aging homosexual becomes too fatigued to cruise. Etc.

To change the shape of metal forms one must apply energy sufficient to rearrange the patterning of molecules. Change the electromagnetic field. So it is with neural imprints. Just as heat is used in metallurgy, so is it necessary to apply massive biochemical energy to loosen the molecular synaptic bonds. Internal stimuli—drugs, trauma, illness, deprivation, shock—can retract the external neural life lines.

Just as heated metal hardens into the new form, so does the re-imprinted nervous system harden into new circuits, freeze back into new membrane forms. We speak here of psychedelic metallurgy, serial re-imprinting, the neurologic craft of recasting the seven minds, recircuiting the bio-electric wiring.

With the present repertoire of Sixth Circuit neurotransmitter drugs it is apparently only possible to re-imprint about once a week. You cannot re-imprint every day. It takes from five to seven days for the new-mind-mold to harden. LSD research indicates that it takes a retractory period of a week for the structure to build up.

If a person had a full-scale LSD re-imprinting experience once a week for forty years, two thousand re-imprintings would be possible. This is to say, two thousand serial-reincarnations could be experienced. It is obvious that even if one played out all

If the recasting of the mind occurs over and over again in the same place with the same set of characters (usually one's larval egos) then the same neural form repeats.

the myths, imprinted all the available roles, focused re-imprints on every sense organ and combination thereof, one would be hard-pressed to find and live out that many reincarnations.

The dismal fact about casual LSD sessions is that the ill-prepared person tends to re-imprint the past conditioned structure; thus charging with new energy the habit-patterns of the old island reality.

It is a fundamental principle of exo-psychology that conditioning centers around the positive and negative poles of the imprint. The imprint-fix is sudden. Post-imprint conditioning, however, takes time and repetition. Around the initial sexual imprint, for example, there builds up, over the years, billions of conditioned associations. This forms the structure of personality.

During a re-imprinting session it is probable that the new imprint includes the old conditioned structure. You re-imprint your spouse, for example. Where new models are imprinted, it is necessary to start building up new circles of conditioned reflexes around the new imprint. This takes time. Some early LSD researchers concluded that a six month waiting period should occur between LSD sessions. In psychological terms, to "work through the new insights." The exo-psychological phrase is "to allow new conditioning to network around the new imprints." But the new imprint model must be present during the re-conditioning.

Neurologic, therefore, requires that one plan one's re-imprinting sessions carefully so that those aspects of previous realities which one wishes to exist in the future reality are present to be imprinted and new models imprinted during the "sensitive" period remain around to allow new conditioned associations to build up around them.

Usually the person re-imprints the old conditioned stimuli.

One often hears the complaint from people who have taken LSD repeatedly that, after a while, the "trips" were the same. Such comments reveal a lack of knowledge of the re-imprinting process. If the recasting of the mind occurs over and over again in the same place with the same set of characters (usually one's larval egos) then the same neural form repeats. This is like having the most precise and expensive photographic equipment and, without moving it, continuing to photograph the same object.

A more thoughtful use of the recasting, reincarnative potentialities of the nervous system was exemplified by the two neurologicians, a newly married couple, who embarked on a psychedelic world tour. The first step was to purchase 'round-the-world air tickets which had to be used within one year. The couple then thought of themselves as orbiting satellites of the planet who had to accomplish the circumnavigation in twelve months.

The procedure was to fly to a country and to enquire as to the "spiritual" center of that nation. In Japan, they were told to go to Kyoto. In India, to Benares. In Greece, to Eleusis. Etc. In Kyoto they asked where the spiritual center, the "soul"

The conflicts, internal and social, which plague larval humanity are often due to discordance among the social-neural-genetic structures.

---

of Kyoto was to be found. They were given many suggestions and visited each center to pick up neuro-genetic vibrations. They spent a week reading about the history, politics, culture, art, myths of Japan and Kyoto. Then they went to the "holiest" place, ingested a Sixth Circuit neuro-active chemical which suspended old imprints and opened the nervous system to new imprints—which in this case were structured by the architecture and regalia of the Emperor's palace. For six hours they absorbed the signals of the place and became neurologically Japanesed.

This is the only way to "see the world"*—to retract the imprint roots and move the unattached nervous system to a new locale to which the neural lines are extended. (See diagrams 13—24.)

Without such flexibility—vulnerability—we can experience nothing outside the membrane that was formed at the time of the last imprinting—which for larvals is the time of adolescence or, in the case of women, their last child-birth. Most world travellers move their robot-bodies from country to country experiencing only symbolic versions of their own home grounds.

Such neural touring is not an end in itself, but a rudimentary training exercise for neurologicians learning how to use the Einsteinian serial possibilities of the brain.

The goal of the neurologician is to increase not just consciousness, but intelligence. Contelligence; to learn how to move and change realities by means of serial re-imprinting. When the nervous system can be used at Einsteinian relativistic speeds, the passive limitations of the nervous system itself become apparent. There are basic genetic dimensions of reality-construction which cannot be changed by re-imprinting. Just as operant conditioning is futile when compared to neural imprinting, so is imprinting superficial when compared with the **Genetic Template**.

We recall: imprinting hooks the bodily-neural equipment to one basic external. The environment (including the body) imprints the nervous system just as film is imprinted in a camera. However, the camera is designed and constructed by **DNA**. The filming process is limited and guided by the structure of the camera.

The most obvious illustration of the relationships among conditioning, imprinting and genetic templating is seen in the sexual response.

DNA, at the time of conception, stamps out the sex and model (zodiac type) of the nervous system.

The nervous system at puberty then imprints the release-stimulus of the sexual machinery. Then social conditioning either supports or ineffectually (and often cruelly) deals with the outcome of this three-layer programming by means of social rewards for virtue and social punishment for "sin."

The conflicts, internal and social, which plague larval humanity are often due

---

*We use the word "see" in the sense of don Juan as contrasted with "looking."

When the nervous system can be used at Einsteinian relativistic speeds, the passive limitations of the nervous system itself become apparent.

to discordance among the social-neural-genetic structures.

It is a simple matter to change conditioned behavior. Just move into a different reward punishment scene.

It requires neurologic know-how to change imprints.

The genetic template, the most powerful determinant of human behavior, cannot, at this time, be changed; it can only be understood and adapted to. When post-larval humanity has evolved to Stage 20 (Genetic Engineering), it will be possible to change genetic pre-disposition.

Neurologic is the science of selective re-imprinting. The use of the nervous system as motion-picture camera. The conscious creation of a sequence of realities.

The structure of the body and of the nervous system is pre-designed by the genetic code.

The code is an amino-acid time-script which contains the multi-billion year sequence of biological evolution. Past and future.

The first task of Life on this planet was to transform the atmosphere. Plant life produces the oxygen atmosphere necessary for later phases of mobile, animal life. This process is called **terraforming.**

When oxygen was produced, the code simply kicked into action the gills, lungs, and oxygen-transporting systems in the body to produce the next phase of evolution.

The evolution of humanity for the billions of years to come may already be pre-programmed in the genetic code, blocked from expression by chemical masking barriers called histones, and turned on by non-histone proteins.*

The blueprint of **DNA** has designed us to move life off the planet and to enter high-velocity, time-relativity states, to attain symbiotic longevity, to construct and direct nuclear-fusion energies which will transport us through the galaxy, and eventually to evolve beyond matter as we now know it.

The intelligent person in the year 1976 has available enough evidence to predict the general course of future evolution, and on the basis of these inevitabilities, to participate in a neurological mutation. It is about time to use our heads; become very contelligent, very rapidly.

One who allows Hirself to be controlled by conditioning or accidental childhood imprinting is accepting robothood. To follow the genetic instruction it is necessary to retract larval imprints and to create new neural realities, new languages based on Einsteinian relativities. Create the future and then imprint it.

Neurologic is the science of selective re-imprinting. The use of the nervous system as motion-picture camera. The conscious creation of a sequence of realities.

It must be remembered, however, that neurologic is a tool for neurogenetics. It is of little use to go on re-imprinting larval realities or somatic realities. The Sixth Circuit is designed for extra-terrestrial existence, for post-human, genetic consciousness. Neurotransmitter drugs, like LSD, are thus seen to be post-larval in function.

The DNA code contains the entire life blueprint—the history of the past and the forecast of the future. The intelligent use of the brain is to imprint the DNA code.

---

*The future of post-larval humanity rests dormant in the unused portion of our genetic code just as the "butterfly" potential lies hidden in the chromosomes of caterpillars.

There is one possibility routinely omitted in future projections—
a sudden global raising of contelligence.

Up until the present, human beings have been neurologically unable to conceive of the future.

This inhibition (Neo-phobia) is genetically imposed. The larval nervous system creates earth-bound realities. For the caterpillar to "think" about flying would be survivally risky. Indeed the caterpillar cannot "think" about flying because it has no wings. We assume that pre-human forms of life have no awareness of time, no ability to look into the future; that mammals operating with the two immediate survival circuits have no conception of the evolutionary plan.*

The key to evolution beyond the larval forms is the understanding and control of time.

The emergence of the laryngeal-manual circuit, the paleolithic unfolding of left-hemisphere symbol-manipulating and logical-ordering allowed humanity to transmit vocal, written and artifactual time-signals across the generations. Operant conditioning, instrumental learning assures the transmission of culture from the past to the present.

Larval time-binding involves very short periods and narrow perspectives. The farmer looks to the next harvest. The politician looks to the next election. The bureaucrat looks forward to payday, to the weekend, to the summer vacation. Parents look to their children.

Larval civilizations operate on the basis of calculated ignorance about the future. The four-brained person does not want to know about the future because it threatens the stability of the reality imprint. Four-brained societies do not want to know about the present, because prospection would lessen the motivation to work blindly towards organized uncertainty.

There is a taboo about future forecast. The book **Future Shock** seems to be more about present shock and describes the terror and confusion created by a world which is different from the past; i.e. different from one's childhood imprint realities. Pro-phobia is so intense that the future cannot be faced in a best-selling book.

Even the scientific groups who try to project the future are curiously unable to foresee an evolving neurological-mutational change. The Club of Rome, the RAND Corporation, Herman Kahn all present statistical extrapolations of material trends of the past projected to the future. Thus we are told that the future will be a global extension of a Swedish Los Angeles. All the current predictions by "futurists" forecast an air-conditioned ant-hill world in which personal freedom, creativity are limited by population pressure, scarcity and restrictive social control.

There is one possibility routinely omitted in future projections—a sudden global raising of contelligence. The "I^2" of S.M.I^2.L.E.

*This assumption may be another anthropocentric myth. The bee-hive, in its elaborate structure, may be a time-binding cultural signal to new generations of bees. U.s.w.

A mutation is always disturbing to the larval culture. No one wants the reality game to become bigger than one's childhood imprints.

The 1960's witnessed a general raising of consciousness, a massive "mind-fission," a widespread retraction of larval imprints. The new realities imprinted were not thoughtfully selected. While there was a "drop-out" away from the artifact-symbols of the parent-culture and a joyful hedonic acceptance of the rapture of direct-sensation ("feel good, stay-high"), there was an unfortunate tendency to reject technology and scientific thinking. The drug-culture of the 1960's wandered around, "spaced out" (this is a good term)', "high," but with no place to go.* One generation too early for interstellar migration.

Into this neural vacuum rushed the "occultists," second hand Karma dealers, Jesus-salesmen, "spiritualists," fad-cultists, astrologers providing occult terms and "other-worldly" explanations for the new transcendental states.

The question of the 1960's was: After retracting imprints from the material culture, where do you go? The answers of the past were: back to Jesus, back to Hassidism, back to India, back to the nature simplicity of the pioneers. The Here and Now of Transcendental Masturbation. The "Me" generation.

The consciousness fads became soothing terrestrial "turn-offs," offering peace of mind, detached serenity, health-foodism, feel-good sensory supermarkets for pre-mature mutants who have no idea of where to go. The water-bed fad is a classic example of pre-mature 5th Circuit mutation, with its hint of zero-gravity sensory freedom.

The hedonic spirit of the 1960's was a manifestation of Stage 13, the receptive, exploratory use of a new neural circuit. It is natural that the first post-larval generation would appear confused, dis-oriented, frivolous, irritatingly vague. The task of the next generation is to learn how to transmit the new experiences, to raise intelligence, to control time, to create extra-terrestrial models based on scientific evidence.

A mutation is always disturbing to the larval culture. No one wants the reality game to become bigger than one's childhood imprints.

The genetic time-table has reached the point where humanity is beginning to understand how the nervous system operates and how robot-synaptic reactions can be suspended. A new level of contelligence is defined.

---

*"Stoned" is a bad term, as is "loaded."

Much of the conflict and confusion which characterizes the current human plight can be gentled and clarified if we accept the fact that we are genetically very different from each other and inexorably pre-programmed by DNA template to evolve in many different directions.

The evolutionary process schedules mutations with a relentless continuity. Every living organism plays a part in the evolutionary design.

There are eight answers to the basic question, "Who am I and where am I going?" In terms of genetic teleology the question is: "In which direction am I mutating?"

The genetic perspective is taboo and frightening because it forces us to face certain embarrassing facts:

1. The human species is an incomplete form which is undergoing dramatic changes.

> The human race (and, indeed, life on this planet) is now at the half-way point. In three billion years we have evolved from uni-celled organisms. In the years to come we shall manifest changes much more dramatic.

2. The rate of evolution is accelerating.

> The human condition is changing at an accelerated rate in terms of physique, neurological function, ecology, density and diversity of population, etc. Consider the human situation 25 years ago, 50 years ago, 100 years ago, 1000 years ago, 10,000 years ago.
>
> Now assume that the same rate of accelerated change continues. How will we evolve in the next 25 years? The next thousand years?

3. The evolutionary process produces an increasing spectrum of differentiations. The present human gene pool will evolve in many different directions. It is probable that hundreds or thousands of new species will evolve from the present human genetic stock.

> The social implications are startling. Of the next hundred persons you meet it is probable that each will evolve into a new species as different from you as the rabbit from the giraffe. About 75 million years ago certain insectivore species (lemurs) contained the seed-source from which the 193 varieties of primates, including the human, were to emerge.

To understand yourself, to understand the human situation it is useful to project a pro-spectus of how the human species is going to evolve.

Much of the conflict and confusion which characterizes the current human plight can be gentled and clarified if we accept the fact that we are genetically very different from each other and inexorably pre-programmed by DNA template to evolve

Each of us transmits a pre-coded design of future organisms very different from current human stock and very different from most other humans.

in many very different directions.

The work of geneticists like Paul, Stein and Kleinsmith suggests that histones mask the half of the DNA code which contains the futique design of the organism. If it were possible for one to pull back the histone curtain and see the blueprint of one's genetic future one would have a most revealing answer to the question, "Who am I and where am I going?" The question must be posed in the first person singular. The error of genetic democracy led Gauguin to ask, "Where did we come from and where are we going?" The question can only be asked, "Where am I going? What genetic futique do I carry in my genes?"

Each of us transmits a pre-coded design of future organisms very different from current human stock and very different from most other humans.

Although the brain receives 100 million impulses a second, mundane consciousness is limited to signals which have been conditioned to one of the four imprinted game-boards.

Exo-psychology holds that the human larval exists in a reality defined by the four survival imprints. Although the brain receives 100 million impulses a second, mundane consciousness is limited to signals which have been conditioned to one of the four imprinted game-boards.

Unconditioned sensations, the raw swirl of an unfiltered reality, exist as background noise.

In communicating with larvals the following points must, therefore, be remembered:

The Larval has no interest in you, you do not exist, unless you can hook into Hir limited reality-island, transmit on Hir narrow mind-band, unless your behavior offers meaning in terms of possible benefit or threat to Hir:

—cellular well being

—emotional-hierarchical status

—artifact manipulation game

—socio-sexual security; domestic reassurance.

All larval interactions are instrumental to one of the four survival attitudes. Larvals are comfortably adapted to this limited four-channel communication, scan automatically for the survival meaning of each stimulus and scuttle by each other like ants, each intent on Hir own "reality"—reacting automatically to relevant cues from others.

Larval communication occurs in terms of four systems, some of which are comprehensible to the entire species, some of which are limited to members of the same cultural-imprint group.

Larvals do not like to receive information unless the facts fit into their 3rd Circuit reality net and immediately reward their emotional status. Democrats were delighted to hear the facts about Nixon, but Republicans were irritated and resistant.

Larvals submit themselves to learn new symbols only under special motivational circumstances where the new connections build on and confirm established systems or give promise of future emotional rewards of which the teacher is model.

Larvals fervently resist new symbols which require a change in their network of associations. This resistance to learning is not psychological; it is neurological and biochemical. New ideas require a change in the wiring of associations and literally cause a "headache."

Communicating with a larval involves building onto the net of associations. You must literally wire each new idea to an existing neural connection. Larvals learn almost no new symbol systems after childhood. They simply add on to or translate into symbols closely connected to the imprint. This accounts for the fact that it takes at least one generation for a new idea to be understood.

It is especially important in communicating with larvals to remember that few symbols now exist for post-larval processes.

Larvals to not like to receive information unless the facts fit into their 3rd Circuit reality net and immediately reward their emotional status.

You cannot use butterfly language to communicate with caterpillars.

Circuit 4 language involves domestic-moral and social values. Here we discover that there are great cultural differences. The basic sperm-egg invitations to orgasm are, of course, global, but the semantics of displacement, inhibition and sublimation become subtle. Indeed, the individuality, intimacy, specificity, inconsistency and volatility of value symbols requires the greatest caution on the part of post-larvals communicating with yokels.

Most larvals live in terror of being seen as sinful or "bad." Constant reassurance is required to maintain the feeling of being socially approved.

In communicating with larvals about sexual, philosophic, or ethical matters, one enters very dangerous terrain. It is almost impossible to discuss philosophy with yokels.

Hypocrisy, unconscious motivation, irrational paradox, need for approval and fear-of-shame dominate every discussion of philosophy-religion.

Larvals may be bored by and may tune-out Circuit 3 symbols which do not fit their imprints and conditioned networks. But Circuit 4 moral symbols or behaviors which are sensed as different trigger off responses of passion and even violence. Because of this philosophic sensitivity, yokel humans tend to avoid philosophic discussions.

This phobia can cause painful reactions when a post-larval attempts to discuss exo-psychology with a mundane.

The reasons for the philosophic phobia:

1. Yokels are ignorant about where life came from, where it is going and why. They are thus terrified by their mortality. Each larval has accepted a flimsy philosophy of life-and-death which SHe does not really believe. Thus the irritation and panic when this basic hypocrisy is threatened by a scientific discussion about life-origin and life destination.

> "The Lutheran church has always been based on the Bible," explains Phil Beck, Production Manager of a local paint company and the superintendent of the Church's Sunday School. "If you start questioning it, where do you stop? If I have to have that much education to sit down and understand Genesis, then why did God let Luther put it in the people's language? At what point do I throw the whole mad mess out the door?"
>
> Time magazine

2. Yokels are robot-slaves to DNA. They blindly labor to perpetuate the species, to breed, to establish domestic arrangements for rearing young and to transmit cultural survival patterns. Any discussion which threatens to expose or question this robothood is extremely painful. The larval cannot tolerate the insight into uneasy areas of uncertainty.

Chapter 26

Discussing exo-psychology with a yokel is like discussing sexual experiences with a pre-adolescent. SHe just can't understand the new reality because Hir neural circuits have not been turned-on. And SHe may turn you in for philosophic child-molesting.

3. Expression and inhibition of sexual behavior is charged with terror, because orgasm and sperm-egg transfer must be domesticated to provide for stable child rearing.

In communicating with larvals one must realize that discussions about life, death, philosophic ultimates, child-rearing, sexuality—are highly individualistic. Reactions to these topics are unpredictable, depending on the intimacy and safety of the situation.

Hypocrisy and violent defensiveness is endemic.

Post-terrestrials, of course, think of little else except what happens after larval imprints are retracted. They are fascinated by communications with their body, their brain, their DNA. Post-larvals emit vibrations which sometimes disturb yokels and other times seduce them into a temporary abandonment of philosophic repressions.

Post-terrestrials are usually funny, erotic, relativistic and philosophically provocative. Yokels can unconsciously sense the difference in a post-terrestrial. It is therefore advisable to be accurate and sensitive when interacting with larvals.

One must be careful not to seduce the yokel into betraying too much truth.

During a philosophic discussion with post-terrestrials, larvals will often get carried away in temporary enthusiasm, confess doubts about their cosmologies, admit ethical relativities and even accept post-larval strivings to leave the planet and escape death.

The post-terrestrial is urged to act with delicacy to avoid any overt or implied criticism of yokel values. It must be remembered that, to the larval, astronomy and genetics involve 4th Circuit ethical issues, which threaten loss of moral approval.

Discussing exo-psychology with a yokel is like discussing sexual experiences with a pre-adolescent. SHe just can't understand the new reality because Hir neural circuits have not been turned-on. And SHe may turn you in for philosophic child-molesting.

Sooner or later the larval is going to realize that, after the exciting flight conversation, SHe is going to remain grounded. At this point the yokel can become passionately moralistic, attacking the post-terrestrial for being elitist, callous to human suffering, anti-human, escapist, or even diabolical.

Immortals must be careful not to wound the sensibilities of mortals.

In particular, one must be diplomatic in discussing the future evolution of the human species. Larval humans naturally believe that evolution has already reached its highest stage with homo sapiens!

Circuit 7 discussions which suggest that evolution is just half-completed, that the human species is fetal and not yet born, that many new superior species will evolve from the present gene pool—are especially wounding to yokel hubris.

Science fiction writers and astronomers have often speculated on the problems of communication between humans and interstellar entities. This problem is no longer academic. It is happening. This book is an example.

---

*The energy-languages of physics, electronics, astronomy, mathematics are post-larval but their relevance to psychology is just now being recognized.

The word "Hippy" is a generic term for the first post-larval stages describing those who genetically (Zodiac type), neurologically (imprint) or historically (hedonic/sub-cultures) get trapped in passive-receptive hedonic life styles. Transcendental masturbation.

Some say that the Post-terrestrial Age was inaugurated in 1926 when a group of German visionaries formed the Verein fur Raumschiftfahrt (Association for Space Travel).

The V.f.R. held meetings, published research papers and performed rocket experiments. The group, unaffiliated with government, operated with the free dedication of a medieval alchemical fraternity. It was disbanded after the accession of Hitler. The goal of the V.f.R. was to arrange chemicals in the correct geometric order to produce the escape velocity to leave the planet.

The exo-psychological goals of V.f.R. were coopted by the Nazis, who used the V-1 and V-2 rockets for larval purposes.

At the same time, atomic physicists were seeking the correct arrangements of pure elements to fission the atom. The success of the Fermi alchemical team in Chicago can be seen as another exo-psychological landmark. The fission of the uranium atom provided the energy source to propel the interstellar, post-Einsteinian rockets which the primitive, chemically-fired Newtonian rockets of von Braun were forecasting.

The neurological revolution of the 1960's provided the biological counterpart of the Einsteinian point of view. The principles of exo-psychology were first presented (1963) in a paper mysteriously titled "The Religious Experience—Its Production and Interpretation."* This essay, which was widely re-printed and anthologized, accurately predicted that the languages and perspectives of science would provide the theology, ontology, cosmology of the future and systematically laid down the foundations of exo-psychology except that the inevitability of extra-planetary migration was not pointed out.

The co-option of nuclear energy, electronics and rocket-research by the military blocked the interstellar perspective and the subsequent 1960's disillusion with science encouraged the vague maxim "look within."

The resulting fascination with oriental quietism, shamanism, and pop-cult yoga produced a systematic anti-intellectualism, a calculated sucrose stupidity, a bland, smiling self-indulgent floating detachment which is personified as "The Hippy" (Stage 13) and "The Yogi" (Stage 14).

"The Hippy" and the "Yogi-Body Engineer" represent the first two of twelve post-terrestrial stages, transitional stages of "wingless butterflies," evolved beyond terrestrial attachments, no longer hooked to mundane symbols. The one-G earth and its survival routines are no longer "real." The Hippie-Zen adept is no longer reflexively reactive to emotional status cues, is unmotivated for dexterous success and unmoved by the virtue-shame systems by which society domesticates its workers;

---

*Leary, Timothy, "The Seven Tongues of God," from The Politics of Ecstasy, New York, College Notes & Texts, 1965.

Chapter 27

A warning is in order. Many five-brained Hippies and Yogis are the most vehement opponents of extra-terrestrial evolution.

but has not yet evolved to the mastery of the newly activated circuits. The true post-terrestrial is shame-less.

The word "Hippy" is a generic term for the first post-larval stages describing those who genetically (Zodiac type), neurologically (imprint) or historically (hedonic/sub-cultures) get trapped in passive-receptive hedonic life styles. Transcendental Masturbation.

The first post-Hiroshima generation has produced millions of Zen "Hippies" who have evolved from the mundane but do not realize that they are extra-terrestrial.

The problem is, in part, one of historical linguistics. The only languages, the only symbols provided by primitive psychology for extramundane experiences were "larval religious." The new reality of the Hippy is symbolized by vague, mystical terms.

A communication vacuum develops. On the one hand, The Hippy, Yogi and Tantric realizes that SHe has evolved somehow. On the other hand, the five-brained person, detached from larval symbols, lurches around grasping at any transcendental straw—magic, occultism, chanting, witchcraft, telepathy, guru-ism, mystical Christianity, Hassidism, experimental evangelism, the endless varieties of oriental charlatanism.

The trap of body-consciousness and sensory consumerism has been well summarized by Federico Fellini:

"People are losing faith in the future. Our [larval] education, unfortunately, molded us for a life that was always tensed towards a series of achievements—school, military service, a career and, as a grand finale, the encounter with the heavenly father. But now that our tomorrows no longer appear in that optimistic perspective, we are left with a feeling of impotence and fear. People who can no longer believe in a "better tomorrow" logically tend to behave with a desperate egotism. They are preoccupied with protecting, brutally if necessary, those little personal gains, one's little body, one's little sensual appetites. To me this is the most dangerous feature of the '70's."

Five-brained persons flopping around sporadically detached from mundane imprints, lacking a vocabulary and a methodology for extra-terrestrial movement, fall back on larval concepts of transcendence. Caterpillar fantasies about what post-larval life will be like.

A warning is in order. Many five-brained Hippies and Yogis are the most vehement opponents of extra-terrestrial evolution. They use three bland sets of cliches to resist practical plans for interstellar migration:

> — Look within. Astral travel, passive changing of consciousness will transport us to the promised land.
> — Return to nature. Back to the paleolithic! Simplify, avoid technology, stalk the wild asparagus, rely on body

The first post-Hiroshima generation was truly a lost generation. Liberated from yokel imprints but with no place to go byond body geography. The cynicism and malaise of the 1970's is the result of this disillusion.

wisdom, organic purity, sensory pleasure.
— **All is one.** The cosmos is a homogeneous mist of flavorless cotton-candy. Exo-psychology and neurogenetics are attacked as unnatural, elitist attempts to differentiate the vanilla-pudding unity of simplistic Hinduism, Buddhism, u.s.w.

Underlying all three of these occultist postures is a revulsion against science, technology, evolution and intellectual competence. Implicit in the occultist theory is the assumption that there is nothing left to learn except to rote-memorize some Hindu chants, to rote-recite some glib theosophical dogmas, to quiet the restless, inquiring mind.

The three stages of the neurosomatic circuit—13. Hippy, 14. Yogi, 15. Tantric— are body-oriented and involve a deliberate symbol stupidity. It is understandable that the five-brained person reacts against the insectoid-cyborg materialism of larval technology, the scientism that produces plastic consumerism, military-industrialism, assembly-line anonomie, and polluted over-population. But the rejection of scientific inquiry becomes a know-nothing smugness. Occultists become long-haired red-necks. The evidence from astronomy, bio-chemistry, genetics, nuclear-physics, defines the true frontier of philosophy and religion. **Scientific American** is more "far-out" than any occult magazine, the Periodic Table of Elements more prophetic than the Tarot deck. The nucleus of the atom is a realm more mysterious and omniscient than any theological fantasy. The cosmology of an expanding-universe-riddled-with-Black-Holes more bizarre than the eschatologies of Dante, Homer and Ramayana.

Despite this noble rejection of the artificial, the Hippie-Yogi-Tantric establishment is an entrenched, self-indulgent block to evolution—a transitional stage preparatory to planetary migration.

We see the limitations of neurosomatic contelligence most clearly in the teachings of don Juan. Castaneda's warrior-sorcerers are admirable in their dignified, humorous, disciplined attempts to retract social imprints. Don Juan has worked out an accurate, metaphorical neurologic. He precisely defines the larval-imprint reality-island (tonal) and the direct experience of the nagual.

But don Juan's philosophy is pessimistic: "There are no survivors on this earth." It fails to evolve to Stage 15 neurosomatic linkage: "And then I was alone," is the bleak conclusion.

The first post-Hiroshima generation was truly a lost generation. Liberated from yokel imprints but with no place to go beyond body geography. The cynicism and malaise of the 1970's is the result of this disillusion.

For these reasons the exo-psychologist must speak with caution in communicating with the members of the "Woodstock" generation. They have imprinted their bodies but are too old and set in their ways (at age 25-35) to receive the neurophysical signals for extra-terrestrial migration.

The pan-spermic U.F.O.s landed three billion years ago and produced the signal, an English translation of which you now hold in your hand.

The past few pages of this transmission have whirled us through several billion years of evolution, introduced us to Higher Intelligence, explained our role as Paleozoic plants, pulled us through larval stages of mammalian body construction, described the robotry of symbol-conditioning, provided the key to sexual male-faction, instructed us in the use of the poly-phase neuroscope (equipped with life-long, re-imprint film), and given us adequate cues to allow us to attain biological immortality and time-dilation.

It is possible that we have already in this introduction transmitted more extra-terrestrial information than is contained in all of the books which have previously been written.

> "But maybe I'm revealing things I shouldn't, don Juan."
> "It doesn't matter what one reveals or what one keeps to oneself," he said. "Everything we do, everything we are rests on our personal power. If we have enough of it, one word uttered to us might be sufficient to change the course of our lives. But if we don't have enough personal power, the most magnificent piece of wisdom can be revealed to us and that revelation won't make a damn bit of difference."

> Carlos Castaneda, Tales of Power, P.16

This book is not for Every Body. The human species is now at a point of genetic fission. Assume that about ninety-three percent of the species is going to adapt to life on the planet. Ecology is the seductive dinosaur science that will lead most of the post-human species to conform to terrestrial conditions, become reasonably comfortable, passive, robot-conditioned cyborg insectoids directed by centralized (ABC, NBC, CIA, MAO, CKB) broadcasting systems. For terrestrial readers this manual outlines the neurological steps necessary to adapt harmoniously to hedonic, five-brained cyborg existence.

This transmission flashes a different signal for the seven percent who we assume are DNA-designed to attain biological immortality, leave the womb-planet, become galactic citizens and fuse with superior interstellar entities.

This manual is not designed for conventional author-reader games. It is a signal for mutation. A test of intelligence. A scan for personal power.

The pan-spermic U.F.O.s landed three billion years ago and produced the signal, an English translation of which you now hold in your hand:

$$S. M. I^2. L. E.$$

PART II

THE PERIODIC TABLE OF ENERGY DEFINES TWENTY-FOUR STAGES OF NEUROLOGICAL EVOLUTION:

Evolutionary Period (Neural Circuit)	Self-oriented Receptive Phase (individualistic, un-attached, hedonistic, asocial, exploratory)	Integrative Phase	Transmission Fusion Phase (hurt, help, social connections, manipulate, communicate, merge)
POST-TERRESTRIAL			
Metaphysiological Neuro-atomic (Interstellar)	22 Neuro-atomic Receptivity	23 Neuro-atomic Intelligence	24 Neuro-atomic Fusion
Neuro-genetic	19 Neurogenetic Receptivity	20 Neurogenetic Intelligence	21 Neurogenetic Fusion Symbiosis
Neurophysical (Interspecies)	16 Neurophysical Receptivity	17 Neurophysical Intelligence	18 Neurophysical Fusion
Neurosomatic	13 Neurosomatic Receptivity	14 Neurosomatic Intelligence	15 Neurosomatic Fusion
TERRESTRIAL			
Sexual-domestic (Homo domesticus)	10 Soc-sexual Receptivity	11 Soc-sexual Domestic Intelligence	12 Soc-sexual Collectivity
L.M. Symbolic (Homo faber)	7 L.M. Symbolic Receptivity	8 L.M. Symbolic Intelligence	9 Symbolic Creativity
Emotion-locomotor (Mammalian)	4 Emotional Self-centered Receptivity	5 Emotional Intelligence	6 Emotional Manipulation
Bio-Survival (Invertebrate)	1 Bio-survival Receptivity	2 Bio-survival Intelligence	3 Bio-survival Fusion

THE TWELVE LARVAL STAGES OF NEURAL EVOLUTION

STAGE 1: BIOSURVIVAL RECEPTIVITY

The unicelled organism and the newly-born mammal float passively, capable only of the reception of viscerotonic stimuli. This is the first stage of contelligence concerned with intake. The attitude is ventral-dorsal. The orientation is endomorphic approach-avoid.

Vegetative contelligence mediates pleasure-pain. Cellular security-danger.

Stage 1 is the basic seed striving towards life. The first inchoate movement towards star-light. Neuro-umbilical lines to the environment have not yet been attached.

This stage is personified in primitive, pre-neurological symbolism as the Zodiac Pisces, the Tarot Fool, the Olympian Hades-Persephone-Pluto-Proserpine.

Definition of self as a viscerotonic entity—a greedy incorporative endomorphic ego-identity.

Every individual human recapitulates in his life the 12 terrestrial stages of organic evolution—from single-cell to centralized socialism.

At the same time each human is genetically programmed to emphasize one of the twelve neurogenetic tasks necessary to keep the human tribal group a complete survival unit. The single human being is an element which is designed to link into a social molecule. There are 12 terrestrial stages of evolution and it is necessary for the primate group to have each survival slot covered. The three bio-survival "cellular" tactics are played out by Pisces, Aries and Taurus. The three mammalian political tactics by Gemini, Cancer, Leo. The three symbol-manipulating functions by Virgo, Libra, Scorpio. The three domesticating tactics by Sagittarius, Capricorn, Aquarius.

Stage 1 performs a visceral cellular function for the human group—at the behavioral level this concerns health and food. Basically, Pisces are visceral organs for the body-politic—as such they provide vegetative wisdom and link to the earliest unicellular consciousness of the species. One often reads about the "deep" mystical quality of Pisces. This is poetic influence to the marine nature of this first and most fusic stage.

It should never be forgotten that the Pisces is an amoeba—very close to hir **DNA,** very in tune with the genetic tape, very soft and moist.

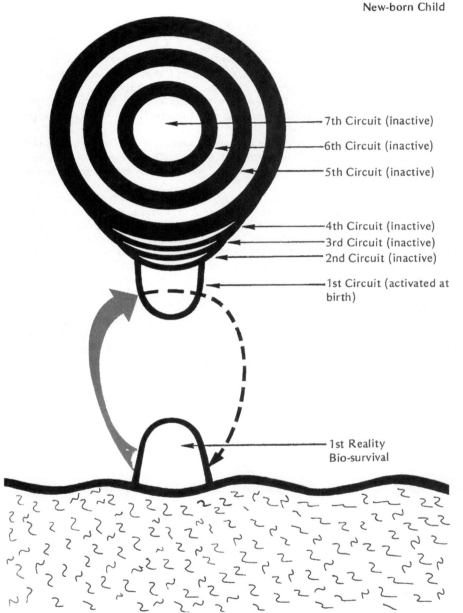

STAGE 1 PISCES
TONIC RECEPTIVITY
New-born Child

— 7th Circuit (inactive)

— 6th Circuit (inactive)

— 5th Circuit (inactive)

— 4th Circuit (inactive)

— 3rd Circuit (inactive)

— 2nd Circuit (inactive)

— 1st Circuit (activated at birth)

— 1st Reality
Bio-survival

Stage 1 begins when the new-born baby receives the first positive stimulus, the breast. Note that Stages 2 and 3 are ready to be activated. This stage, phylogenetically, is unicellular. The human who is genetically wired to play this role in the 12-unit human group is called Pisces; and all through life tends to emphasize or fall back on Stage 1 marine behavior.

STAGE 2: BIOSURVIVAL INTELLIGENCE

In species evolution Stage 2 is the muscular bony marine organism, equipped with a multi-neuron nervous system capable of memory, integration and evaluation of stimuli, and capable of attack-approach in addition to ingest-approach.

In individual development Stage 1 is the neonate after the first imprint has been formed—thus able to distinguish the basic safe (maternal) and the basic dangerous (non-maternal).

The Aries is classically described as a young immature Zodiac stage. This reflects the self-directed, infantile, driving nature of Stage 2. The Ram, however, is not the correct genetic sign. The Aries is in its playful moods a mer-man-mermaid and in hir aggressive moods a shark.

The attitude is ventral-dorsal. Whereas the Stage 1 organism can only receive or flee, using amoebic pseudopod flow, the Stage 2 organism is capable of selective aggressive biting-stinging behavior in addition to sucking, incorporation, digestion etc.

The Stage 1 amoeboid organism has not developed a polor asymmetry. The Stage 2 organism has evolved to an asymmetrical polar structure, usually with a head (hypostomes and tentacles) and a foot (peduncle and basal disk). The nervous system is a simple net that is densest in the head region. This polarity is not oriented to a gravity-determined vertical dimension, but a forward-backward dimension. Differentiation into cell types has occurred.

The human infant is the neurological equivalent of a marine organism. The vegetative circuit of the infant imprints the basic reality, the first attachment of the organism to the environment. This stage is personified as the Zodiac Aries, the Tarot Magus, and the Olympian Neptune-Amphitrite.

BIO-SURVIVAL INTELLIGENCE
(New-born Child
Somatic-greedy-Ego)

7th Circuit (inactive)

6th Circuit (inactive)

5th Circuit (inactive)

4th Circuit (inactive)

3rd Circuit (inactive)

2nd Circuit (inactive)

1st Circuit (2 stages
active)

1st Reality
Bio-survival

Stage 2 begins shortly after birth when the baby begins to discriminate, remember, select, integrate bio-survival behavior. Note that Stage 1 has been activated but Stage 3 has not (dotted line). This stage, phylogenetically, is marine. The human who is wired to play this role in the 12-unit human group is called Aries, and all through life tends to favor or fall back on Stage 2 shark-like behavior.

STAGE 3: BIOSURVIVAL FUSION

In species evolution Stage 3 is the amphibian.

In the development of the individual Stage 3 is the infant linked neurologically with the Mother. This stage introduces the first social, inter-organism linkage—maternal-infant. The synergistic profit from this viscerotonic fusion is incalculable. Instead of devouring or fighting each other, for the first time two organisms connect neurologically for mutual survival. The communication is viscerotonic, cellular.

In the human this stage is the endomorphic, flesh-connection, personified by the Zodiac Taurus, Tarot Empress, Olympian Demeter-Ceres, Dionysus.

The Taurus template is often symbolized as the Bull. This is inaccurate and represents the male chauvinism which plagues most occult and astrological systems. Taurus is better described as the cow-calf linkage—although sea-cow, frog, octopus are more appropriate totems. Taurus is an infantile sign—greedy, sensual, unfolding. The fact that adult Taurans are greedy for more complex materials should not disguise the fact that they are at the same time very maternal and very dependent.

STAGE 3 TAURUS
BIO-SURVIVAL VISCEROTONIC FUSION (SYNERGISTIC)
(Infant-Mother Linkage)
(Somatic Politician)

7th Circuit (inactive)

6th Circuit (inactive)

5th Circuit (inactive)

4th Circuit (inactive)
3rd Circuit (inactive)
2nd Circuit (inactive)

1st Circuit (all 3 stages active)

1st Reality
Bio-survival

Stage 3 is initiated when the infant links with the maternal life-giving person. This stage, phylogenetically, is invertebrate. The human who is genetically wired to play this role is called Taurus; and all through life tends to emphasize material comfort and vegetative satisfaction.

STAGE 4: EMOTION-LOCOMOTION RECEPTIVITY

The Second Circuit emerged when living organisms left the water, developed backbones, learned to master gravity, control territory and establish dominance hierarchies.

In the individual's development the Second Circuit is activated when the young child begins to crawl and toddle.

Stage 4 is the exploratory, self-centered period during which the child begins to master gravity, coordinate mobility muscles, move upwards against gravity—but before cooperative emotional distinctions are made. The child defines a new self, musculotonic, able to move agilely on the ground.

Phylogenetically this stage produces animal forms which operate as "emotional loners," surviving without group cooperation.

This stage is personified in primitive psychology as Gemini, High (Sly) Priestess, Hermes-Mercury (female—Mercuria, Hermia).

The Zodiac symbol for this stage is Twins—an ambiguous and confusing label. Gemini is better described by such animals as otters, jackals, foxes, rodents—creatures who survive by means of stealth, rapidity, agility.

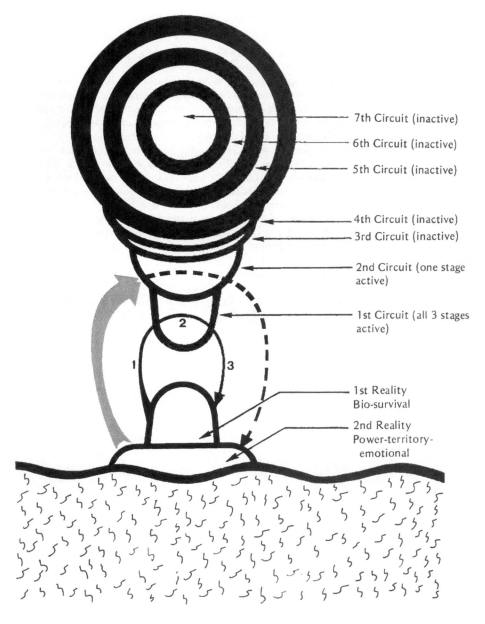

7th Circuit (inactive)

6th Circuit (inactive)

5th Circuit (inactive)

4th Circuit (inactive)

3rd Circuit (inactive)

2nd Circuit (one stage
active)

1st Circuit (all 3 stages
active)

1st Reality
Bio-survival

2nd Reality
Power-territory-
emotional

Stage 4 begins when the child begins to crawl and walk. The neural wiring of the muscular circuit is turned-on. The receptive stage of the 2nd Circuit involves mobility,
evasion. This stage is mammalian. The human who is wired to favor this role is called
Gemini and all through life tends to emphasize cover-up and agile mobility.

STAGE 5: EMOTIONAL INTELLIGENCE

The musculotonic Second Circuit is upward and mobile—programmed to avoid helplessness, master territory, attain autonomy.

Gravity and territory are basic factors in the evolution of life. A new neural circuit is activated to facilitate the transition from marine to land-life. Survival on land involves control of turf; the strength or cunning to hold territory for food and for breeding. Complex strategies are developed by the various mammalian species, muscular power, speed, camouflage, evasion—all designed to get-out-from-under.

As the human child begins to walk SHe begins to sense the complex web of emotional hierarchy which comprises the Second Reality of mammalian Politics. The selection of the appropriate emotional-political response is determined by the Second imprint. There are times to approach, avoid, attack, dominate, submit, give or take. To learn the complex nuances of pecking order, dominance hierarchy, territorial status is survivally important for the mammal and for the young child. Motor-muscular responses are no longer automatic approach-or-avoid tactics. Incoming signals are scanned, evaluated, interpreted by the jumpy, nervous Second brain and the appropriate emotional response selected.

This stage is personified by the Zodiac Cancer, the Tarot Emperor, the Olympian Hestia.

The Zodiac symbol for this stage is the Crab. A better neurogenetic totem for this stage is a centaur with the face of Leonid Brezhnev, or perhaps a cigar-smoking dinosaur.

STAGE 5 CANCER
NEURO-MUSCULAR INTELLIGENCE
(Child learning to control gravity-territory)
(Mammalian brain)

7th Circuit (inactive)

6th Circuit (inactive)

5th Circuit (inactive)

4th Circuit (inactive)

3rd Circuit (inactive)

2nd Circuit (2 stages active)

1st Circuit (all 3 stages active)

1st Reality Bio-survival

2nd Reality Power-territory-emotional

Stage 5 begins when the walking child begins to understand and evaluate mobility and muscular actions in terms of control, status and freedom. This stage is mammalian. The human who is wired (genetically) to favor this role is called Cancer and throughout life tends to emphasize possession, control, centrality of position.

/ 85

STAGE 6: EMOTIONAL FUSION

The next stage of neuro-muscular adaptation involves group communication and cooperation among members of the insect colony, the primate troop, the beaver colony, the herd, the human group.

Intricate social networks emerge. The individual's survival depends upon discriminating social differences and fitting into the social web. The organism inhibits some automony to adjust to the group. Division of emotional role, social fusions appeared in human evolution when the pre-humanoid primates formed hunting packs and hierarchical social units.

The Second Circuit imprint determines the emotional style, the interpersonal ego which persists into maturity.

This stage is personified by Leo, High Priest, Apollo/Amazonia. The mammalian politician.

The neurogenetic totem is Lion-Lioness. The 5th Stage—Cancer—grabs and holds. The 6th Stage Leo manages—dominates through political linkage.

NEURO-MUSCULAR LINKAGE
(Child Imprinting a Dominance Role)
(Mammalian Politician)

7th Circuit (inactive)

6th Circuit (inactive)

5th Circuit (inactive)

4th Circuit (inactive)

3rd Circuit (inactive)

2nd Circuit (all 3 stages active)

1st Circuit (all 3 stages active)

1st Reality Bio-survival

2nd Reality Power-territory-emotional

Stage 6 is activated when the child establishes Hir methods of domination, makes the group-herd linkage for maintaining territory. This stage, phylogenetically, is that of the social animal, the mammalian politician. The human who is genetically wired to play this role is called Leo; and all through life emphasizes social dominance.

STAGE 7: RECEPTIVITY OF LARYNGEAL-MANUAL SYMBOLS

The Third Circuit emerged phylogenetically when the left hemisphere of the cortex developed its specialized function of mediating dexterity, manipulation of artifacts and management of the nine muscles of the larynx which perform symbolic speech. The paleolithic homanid.

The first stage of symbolic intelligence is receptive, imitative, self-centered. The paleolithic finding bones and stones. The child accepting the symbols presented by adults, mimicking. The adult who uses symbols irrationally, as magical repetitious tokens.

At this first symbolic stage there is no inventiveness, no conceptual thinking, no engineered manipulation. Repetition is the mode of thought and action. Satisfaction comes from grasping the given symbol. Rote performance.

Primitive human social groups do not progress beyond this stage of symbolic passivity. Certain individuals, because of genetic template or imprint, do progress beyond this mental level.

Stage 7 repetition of symbols is flamboyantly illustrated by intellectuals and philosophers who learn how to reproduce words and then repeat them dexterously— a simple feat of muscular manipulation which is most impressive to themselves and others.

Stage 7 has been personified as Virgo, Tarot Adolescent Lovers, and Olympian Diana-Minerva-Narcissus-Hyacinthus-Echo.

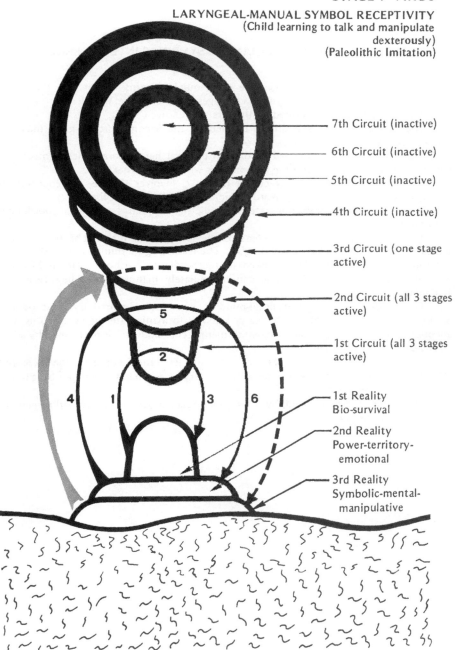

STAGE 7 VIRGO
LARYNGEAL-MANUAL SYMBOL RECEPTIVITY
(Child learning to talk and manipulate
dexterously)
(Paleolithic Imitation)

———— 7th Circuit (inactive)

———— 6th Circuit (inactive)

———— 5th Circuit (inactive)

————4th Circuit (inactive)

———— 3rd Circuit (one stage
active)

———— 2nd Circuit (all 3 stages
active)

———— 1st Circuit (all 3 stages
active)

——— 1st Reality
Bio-survival

———2nd Reality
Power-territory-
emotional

——— 3rd Reality
Symbolic-mental-
manipulative

Stage 7 is activated when the child begins to talk and manipulate artifacts. Note that
Stages 8 and 9 are ready to be activated. This stage phylogenetically is early primate.
The human who is genetically wired to play this role is called Virgo.

STAGE 8: LARYNGEAL-MANUAL SYMBOLIC INTELLIGENCE

As the Third Circuit emerges the child quickly learns to perceive the world through manipulations of the laryngeal cartilages and the manual muscles.

The infant's reality is defined by the First Vegetative Circuit.

The pre-verbal child's reality is defined by the Second Circuit—gross musculature mediating locomotion and ascension.

The Third Circuit is located in the left-cerebral hemisphere which controls the nine muscles of the larynx and the fine-muscles which govern dexterity.

The receptive stage of this circuit (Stage 7) involves the passive repetition of laryngeal and manual sequences. Word magic. Superstitious symbolism.

Stage 8—the third brain integrates symbolic-signals, relates, evaluates, coordinates symbolism.

The importance and pervasiveness of the laryngeal-manual cerebrotonic reality has not been understood by psychologists. The technological human is almost entirely surrounded by artifacts. Placed naked in the wilderness without artifacts SHe can exist only to the extent that SHe can immediately manufacture a new reality of artifacts.

The operation of the laryngeal-mind is even more ignored by philosophers. Sanity and survival depend on the learned ability to manipulate the vocal cords with adequate skill. All thought and almost all mental consciousness is **performed** by silent laryngeal muscle movement.

The Eighth Stage of species and individual evolution concerns the executive mastery of these two precise muscle systems—larynx and hand—mediated by the left hemisphere of the brain.

This stage is personalized by Libra, Olympian Psyche-Mnemosyne/Prometheus and the Tarot Chariot.

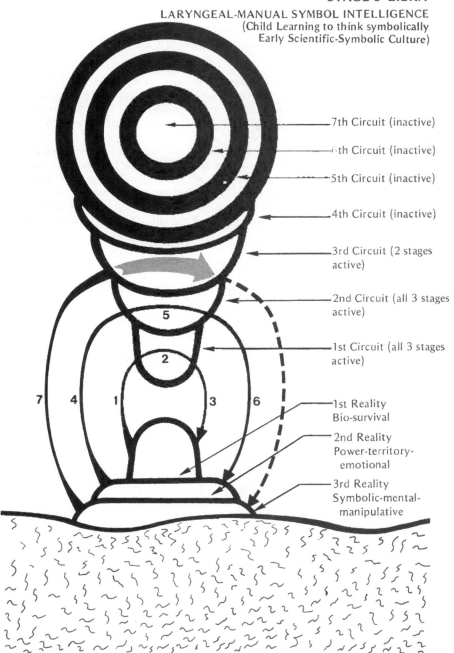

STAGE 8 LIBRA
LARYNGEAL-MANUAL SYMBOL INTELLIGENCE
(Child Learning to think symbolically
Early Scientific-Symbolic Culture)

7th Circuit (inactive)

6th Circuit (inactive)

5th Circuit (inactive)

4th Circuit (inactive)

3rd Circuit (2 stages
active)

2nd Circuit (all 3 stages
active)

1st Circuit (all 3 stages
active)

1st Reality
Bio-survival

2nd Reality
Power-territory-
emotional

3rd Reality
Symbolic-mental-
manipulative

Stage 8 is activated when the child begins to relate symbols, "think." This stage phylogenetically is primate. The human who is wired, genetically, to play this role is called
Libra.

STAGE 9: SYMBOLIC MANIPULATION

The development of L.M. intelligence involves communication of symbols—symbol inventiveness and creativity. The breaking-up of routinized symbol sequences and the creating of new symbols and symbol connections. The Bronze-Iron Age hominid is the prototype. Chopping, mining, melting the natural forms. The creative use of fire. Creative craftsmanship.

At certain epochs of history, social groups and individuals have specialized in fissioning static, routinized symbol sequences and creating new fusions. Each individual during the pre-adolescent stage develops Hir own style of communication. While some are genetically pre-programmed to play this symbol-rearranger role in the larval community, each individual passes through this stage in the cycle of personal evolution. This stage is personalized by Scorpio, Tarot Strength, and Greco-Roman Minerva-Athena-Vulcan-Theseus.

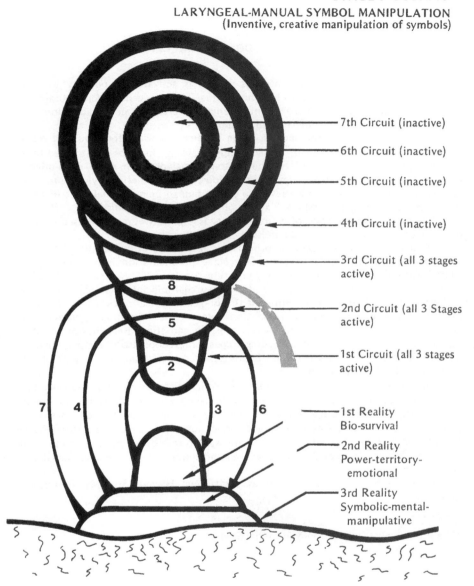

STAGE 9 SCORPIO
LARYNGEAL-MANUAL SYMBOL MANIPULATION
(Inventive, creative manipulation of symbols)

7th Circuit (inactive)

6th Circuit (inactive)

5th Circuit (inactive)

4th Circuit (inactive)

3rd Circuit (all 3 stages active)

2nd Circuit (all 3 Stages active)

1st Circuit (all 3 stages active)

1st Reality
Bio-survival

2nd Reality
Power-territory-emotional

3rd Reality
Symbolic-mental-manipulative

Stage 9 is activated when the primate begins to invent symbols and create new connections. This stage, phylogenetically, is usually considered primitive, pre-civilized human. The human who is genetically wired to play this role in the 12 unit human group is called Scorpio.

STAGE 10: SEXUAL-DOMESTIC RECEPTIVITY*

The Fourth Circuit of the nervous system is activated at puberty when the anatomy of the body matures to breeding status. The new generotonic neural wiring mediates a more complex level of contelligence and creates a new reality dominated by sperm-egg urgency and domesticated sublimations of sexuality.

In the evolution of the species, Stage 10 emerges when the Iron Age technology makes possible mobility of armed bands (traveling in ships constructed by the use of metal tools) which initiates the proto-imperial predator state—male-oriented, macho, free-booting, warlike, lawless, rapacious. This Homeric phylogenetic stage, of course, is recapitulated in adolescence of the human being. Females, at this stage, are sex-objects, pretty possessions, Playboy pin-ups, Venus-Aphrodites.

The first adolescent stage of neurosexuality is explorative, receptive, self-centered, self-defined, orgasm-oriented and narcissistically undomesticated.

During this stage the sexual imprint is laid down, the Fourth reality defined and a sexual-impersonation role selected. Sex-role experimentation is passionately conducted. Contelligence is obsessed with courting rituals, display, sexual exploration—or, if the genetic template is neuter and/or the sexual imprint renunciate, the energy is diverted towards intense commitment to non-genital social roles, adolescent idealizations, obsessive anti-sexuality, romantic displacements. A confusing aspect of the pre-procreative sexual stage is that social pressure can stimulate behavior for which the nervous system is not geared, leading to passionless copulatory role-playing on the part of the genetically neutered and highly charged asceticism on the part of those whose sexuality is socially inhibited.

The Fourth Circuit defines soc-sex roles which differ as much as the caste types in an insect colony. A large percentage of humans are not designed for pro-creation and parenthood but neurogenetically wired to play other domesticated roles. Phylogenetically, the Fourth Circuit emerged when homo sapiens evolved from the late Bronze-Iron-Age social group in which there was no role differentiation among males or among females (except for power-status) and developed the complex social structures of urban civilization.

Stage 10 has been personified as Sagittarius, Hermit, and Mars-Venus-Ares-Aphrodite.

---

*The Individualist; called Hooligan by the Soviets.

STAGE 10 SAGITTARIUS
SOCIAL-SEXUAL ROLE SELECTION

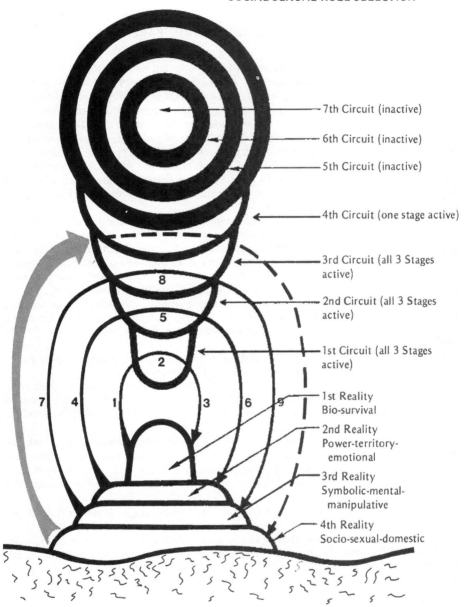

- 7th Circuit (inactive)
- 6th Circuit (inactive)
- 5th Circuit (inactive)
- 4th Circuit (one stage active)
- 3rd Circuit (all 3 Stages active)
- 2nd Circuit (all 3 Stages active)
- 1st Circuit (all 3 Stages active)
- 1st Reality Bio-survival
- 2nd Reality Power-territory-emotional
- 3rd Reality Symbolic-mental-manipulative
- 4th Reality Socio-sexual-domestic

Stage 10 begins at adolescence when the sexual machinery is turned-on and the 4th Circuit is activated. At this time the sexual imprint is made; a sex-role impersonation is developed. Phylogenetically this circuit defines the Homeric Ape, the Civilized Larval. The human who is genetically wired to play this role is called Sagittarius.

STAGE 11: SEXUAL DOMESTICATION, PARENTHOOD*

The Fourth Circuit creates the parent-family-oriented social reality.

When this circuit is activated the soc-sex imprint blindly registers the object in the environment which becomes both trigger and target of the sexual domestic impulse.

A complex genetic pre-programming defines the kind and amount of soc-sex types necessary for the preservation of the extended-family. Just as the "DNA brain" of the insect colony activates the appropriate number of workers, drones, warriors, so does the "species brain" of homo sapiens produce the breeding types of humans.

Larval humans are unaware both of their function as "seed-carriers" and of the genetic role they are programmed to play. Some are sexually neuter, others designed for parenthood. It is a simple matter to identify the soc-sex role of humans even as early as the onset of puberty.

The variety of genetic and neural human types causes considerable confusion and social conflict. Laws, ethical codes and educational methods assume a homogeneity which does not exist. Human society is a Darwinian jungle inhabited by a broad evolutionary spectrum. The Fourth imprint channels and conceals these genetic differences by hooking the nervous system to standard social models. The human is domesticated via imprint to respond in conventional family patterns—including aunts-uncles, grandparents, etc. At the time of impregnation, powerful bio-chemical and neurological changes occur which produce nesting and child-protective responses. Even those who are not parents are programmed to value and moralize the welfare of children.

The 11th Stage of neural evolution (Parental-Domestication) is personified by Capricorn, the Wheel of Life, and Juno-Hera-Jupiter-Jove.

While the 11th Stage is inclusively domestic—involving all the parental roles of the extended family—the slot is basically female. Historically the family-centered society replaced the male dominated predator state with the more gentle intercourse of trade and family-model companies.

In this connection it is useful to recall that each neurogenetic slot is basically male or female. While every developing human passes through each stage—effectively or neurotically—there is a basic, rhythmic alternation between male and female stages.

An interesting helical unfolding of alternate sex roles is involved in neurogenetic evolution.

The male Pisces is the male version of the female stage. A female Leo is the feminine, Amazon version of the male stage.

We note the difficulty in finding Greco-Roman divinities for the male counterpart of Pisces—Persephone, Taurus—Demeter, Cancer—Lares-Penates, Virgo—Diana, Scorpio—Athena. And we note the similar problem in labelling the female counterpart of Aries—Neptune, Gemini—Mercury, Leo—Apollo, Libra—Prometheus.

---

*The Bourgeois Human.

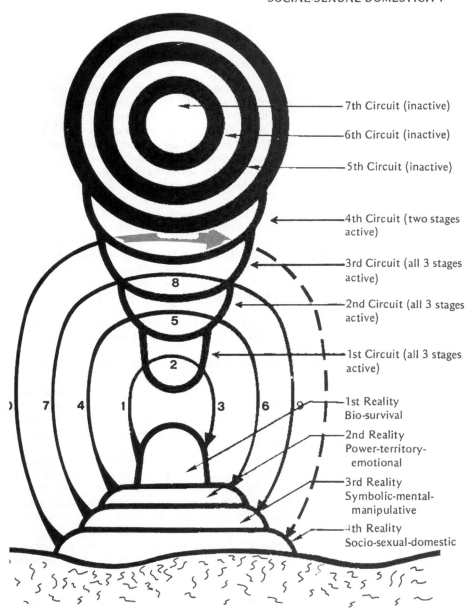

STAGE 11 CAPRICORN
SOCIAL-SEXUAL DOMESTICITY

7th Circuit (inactive)

6th Circuit (inactive)

5th Circuit (inactive)

4th Circuit (two stages active)

3rd Circuit (all 3 stages active)

2nd Circuit (all 3 stages active)

1st Circuit (all 3 stages active)

1st Reality Bio-survival

2nd Reality Power-territory-emotional

3rd Reality Symbolic-mental-manipulative

4th Reality Socio-sexual-domestic

Stage 11 is activated when the nervous system imprints a Sperm-egg Sexual Impersonation. Phylogenetically this stage defines the family-oriented civilization which precedes the collectivist state. The human who is genetically wired to play this role is called Capricorn.

STAGE 12: COLLECTIVE SOCIALIZATION [INSECTOID]

Collective socialization is obviously the most effective survival device.

Two brained mammals rear their offspring to maturity at which time they become independent rivals. Three brained primates live in packs or groups with rudimentary social organization and sexual differentiation of role. Insects and homo sapiens have developed an invincible adaptive mechanism—the centralized society in which the fate of the individual is subordinate to the welfare of the collective. Both the human individual and the species evolve from Stage 10, pre-parental, self-indulgent, undomesticated predator sexuality, through Stage 11, parental responsibility of the family-centered society, to Stage 12, in which the sexually energized domestic instinct is broadened and sublimated from the family to insectoid society at large—centralized socialism.

Stage 10 sexuality is self-oriented and was developed historically in the Mediterranean cultures—Hellenistic, Arab, Catholic—feudalistic, aristocratic—in which the male uses power for sexual gratification and women are property. This "adolescent" stage of sexual-socialization is at the same time both luxurious-licentious and sternly moral. It is no accident that the Middle-sea cultures produce both Arab-sensuality and Islamic prudishness, Hellenistic hedonism and pre-Christian asceticism, Catholic monasticism and Latin sexuality. The profligate King and the renunciate priesthood. Women as whores or saints.

Stage 11 sexual-domestication is based on the family and developed historically in Northern Europe as the middle-class alliance of brotherhood, fraternity. Incest taboos inhibit free sexuality among siblings.

However appealing this evolutionary period with its democracy, free enterprise competition, parliamentarianism, consumerism, property-rights—it is obviously a less efficient and less successful form of social survival than Stage 12 insectoid collectivism.

Those who have been imprinted with Mediterranean or middle-class democratic models are incapable of understanding the power of the collective-imprint. The deeprooted reverence which the Mediterranean feels for himself, and the Stage 11 Domestic for family, is replaced by the Stage 12 devotion to the state.

In the collective society, individualism (called "hooliganism" by the Soviets), romantic love, and familial loyalty (called "bourgeois" by the Soviets) are considered evil and treasonable. The child whose nervous system develops in socialist-collectives invests the state with the sublimated sexuality which in pre-socialist societies is fragmented into individual and familial connections. This is to say, the courting activities—dress, grooming, ritualistic expressions of passion, music, romantic symbolism formerly designed to attract a member of the opposite sex are now directed towards winning the approval of the state. Virtue is not in parental terms, but in duty to the collective.

Socialist and communist states are prudish and inhibitory about boy-girl sexuality for powerful neurological reasons. The mating and domestic instincts are co-opted by the state. The nesting behavior, the protective husbandry reflexes now cherish, feed, support and defend the state.

Stage 12 socialist-idealistic sublimation of sexual energies is the final culmination of larval evolution. All the slogans are correct. The organized meek shall inherit the earth. The masses will rule the planet. Insectoid-socialism will dominate.

Stage 12 is personified in the Zodiac Aquarius, Tarot Justice, and the Olympian Themis-Nemesis.

Stage 12 contelligence involves a detachment from many of the instinctual neural reflexes which have provided security to developing larvals. The socialist imprint requires that the individual and the family yield to the state the controls and freedoms which have assured survival to the individual in the past. The Second Circuit animal imprint to the home-ground-territory is suspended. No more private property. All the land belongs to the state; or in corporate-capitalist societies the tract-house belongs to the bank and the individual is frequently transferred by the company thus severing the connection to turf. Third Circuit L.M. symbols are standardized. The socialist child cannot "make up hir mind" in the educational context of a wide variety of laryngeal-manual muscle systems. The inventive, creative mind disappears. Cultural life-style, sex-role, private modes of sublimated expression which give the illusion of uniqueness to the domesticated larval become homogenized (beautiful word) to Soviet or television uniformity.

Although this insectoid, mono-cultism is horrifying in its subordination of earlier human values [individual and familial], Stage 12 is actually an inevitable evolutionary step. Each new circuit of the nervous system leads to a higher level of union-linkage:

1. unicellular forms cluster into multi-celled organisms
2. organisms cluster into territorial packs, herds, groups
3. tool-making homanids cluster into craft-guilds, trade-unions, symbol-sharing collectives
4. families expand into giant centralized states

The insectoid-state-collectives are a necessary step in larval evolution. Only the centralized state can harness the technology to make possible the next evolutionary step— migration from the planet. It is necessary to sever the robot-mammalian-connections to the plot of personal territory, to local symbol fetishes, to personal sexual roles, to family allegiances—in order to be free to mutate. The bird must retract his imprint to the nest in order to migrate south.

The four larval imprints can be seen as landing pods, neural extensions to the placental planet, neuro-umbilical cords to assure fetal survival. The genetic engineering is simple to understand. DNA, at birth, lands on the new planet in an infant's body and sends out, in sequence, four life-support systems:

— ventral dorsal
— muscular
— manipulative (laryngeal-manual muscular)
— sexual-affiliative.

When the four-brained larval has evolved to the level of contelligence which can organize the technology necessary to metamorphize into migratory flight, it is obviously necessary to withdraw the four neuro-umbilical cords from the earth environment. Larval imprints must be retracted. Robot reactions to earth-environment must be internalized. This process has been called "dropping out."

Here is the paradox of technological mysticism; to go out to the stars, one must go within and master one's own body, one's own brain, one's own DNA.

To leave the womb-planet, WoMan must withdraw attachments to external stimuli. The mystical injunction to sever materialistic desire, to cut-off worldly ambition, can now be restated neuro-genetically.

The directive becomes: attain conscious-control of the four new neural processes which were formerly blocked by the four imprinted attachments.

The four post-terrestrial circuits are time-versions of the four larval imprints.

The four larval circuits mediate muscular control of space-territory.

The four post-larval circuits mediate neurological control of "time-territory."

The first larval circuit blindly imprints the vegetative body to external endomorphic nourishment. The Fifth (Neurosomatic) Circuit, which is the first post-larval, frees the body from its environmental imprint. To exist in extra-terrestrial, zero-G space the body must be experienced and controlled as a time ship independent of earth-connections.

Stage 1 infantile floating is recapitulated in Stage 13, neurosomatic passive receptivity. The turned-on Hippie is the extra-terrestrial "neo-nate."

Stage 2, bio-vegetative intelligence is recapitulated in Stage 14, neuro-somatic intelligence.

Stage 3, bio-survival linkage is recapitulated in Stage 15, neurosomatic fusion.

The book **Eight Calibre Brain** specifies how Second Circuit muscular control of territory is replaced by neurological speed, mobility, Einsteinian agility and power; Circuit 2 struggle for territorial power is matched by Circuit 6 control of reality. And Third-Circuit invention and creation (of L.M. symbols) is replaced by the "genius" of genetics. Circuit 3 becomes Circuit 7. Life is an organic evolving amino-acid symbol system; the alphabet of DNA, itself composed by atomic intelligence.

The horrible homogeneity of the Stage 12 mass-cult frees the larval nervous system for migration. Only the organized ant-colony could have produced Almagordo, V-2, Sputnik and Apollo 13. The horror of the corporate socialist state is not the collectivization per se, but that the goals and ends to which it is directed are larval-materialist.

The Chinese-Russian and American mass-cults are repulsive because the ideals are chauvinist, competitive, imperialist, territorial. The demoralization and malaise of the great technological empires is due to the purposeless materialism. The boredom and frustration of insectoid larval cultures-over-population: no frontiers to explore, nothing to do except lurch from crisis-to-scandal or provoke quarrels along the Sino-soviet border or the Golan Heights.

Homo sapiens is on the threshold of discovering that expanding contelligence is the goal of the trip. That pleasure resides not in external-materials but inside the time envelope of the body; that power resides not in muscles and muscle-surrogate machines, but in the brain; that the evolutionary blueprint is to be found in the genetic scriptures; that Higher Intelligence is to be found in the galaxy.

Within a decade (i.e. by 1986) the first male-female migrations into space will occur. The neuro-political impact of this domestic migration will be profound. Humans today can look to the sky and know that American male warrior-astronauts walked on the moon, that Pioneer probes have orbited Jupiter. But the effect is uninspiring. Astronauts were robots with whom humans could not identify.

But when humans look to the sky and realize that seed has been sent, that men and women have left the planet for good and are living, making love, cooking meals, and having children—seeking new forms of existence in extra-terrestrial space—the metamorphosis will be a neurological reality. The great mutation will have begun.

The goals of Stage 12 mass-cult will become the exploration of new worlds, seeking, not gold, but the next level of contelligence.

The first step in evolving to post-larval existence is neurosomatic contelligence—resurrection of the body, mastery of the body as time-ship independent of larval imprints. Circuit 5.

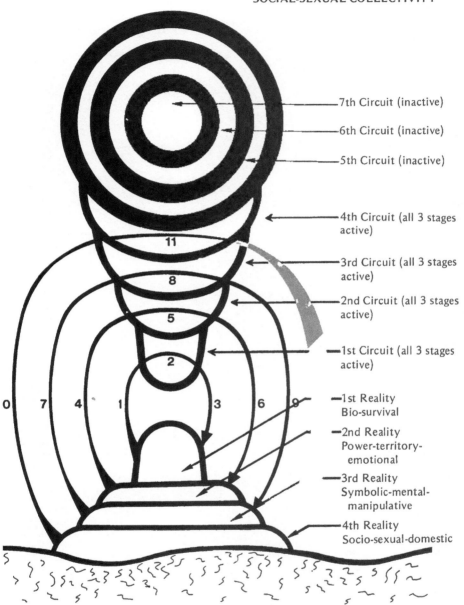

STAGE 12 AQUARIUS
SOCIAL-SEXUAL COLLECTIVITY

7th Circuit (inactive)

6th Circuit (inactive)

5th Circuit (inactive)

4th Circuit (all 3 stages active)

3rd Circuit (all 3 stages active)

2nd Circuit (all 3 stages active)

1st Circuit (all 3 stages active)

1st Reality Bio-survival

2nd Reality Power-territory-emotional

3rd Reality Symbolic-mental-manipulative

4th Reality Socio-sexual-domestic

Stage 12 is activated when the nervous system imprints society as its Social-sexual Connection. Phylogenetically this stage defines the Collectivist Society, the Socialist State. The human who is genetically wired to play this role is called Aquarius.

THE TWELVE EXTRA-TERRESTRIAL STAGES OF EVOLUTION

As we have seen, the first stage of each new evolutionary cycle means liberation from the preceding linkage. Each third stage of each newly emerged neural circuit involves a new, more complex linkage. The activation of the Fifth Circuit, the first post-larval, is an event of great psychological significance and revelation. The umbilical imprints are retracted. A new reality is experienced—a widened perspective in which the previous imprinted survival realities are seen as robot-fractions, no longer limiting or binding. This experience has been described in countless reports by mystics, poets, psychedelic adepts, occultists, and drug users in the language of larval cultures, necessarily vague and subjective.

The basic facts are:

1. that there are other levels of reality beyond the socially conditioned,
2. that these experiences are measurable, predictable, neurological events, and
3. that they can be best understood and classified in terms of the neurotransmitter bio-chemicals which induce them and the circuits of the nervous system which are activated by them.

While there are many systems for classifying the varieties of transcendental experience, exo-psychology defines three post-larval levels of contelligence which are defined by anatomical structure. (Circuit 8 is metaphysiological.)

5. **Neurosomatic Contelligence**: body reality. The reception, integration and transmission of sensory-somatic signals,

6. **Neurophysical Contelligence**: located in the cerebral cortex mediating the reality of the brain, electromagnetic signals,

7. **Neurogenetic Contelligence**: transceiving DNA signals via RNA.

The three circuits can be defined not only in terms of neuro-anatomy and by the phenomenological content of the signal-units experienced, but also by the neurotransmitter substances which activate them.

Larval psychology has not been able to explain the nature or purpose of the three exo-psychological levels of contelligence because they are irrelevant, confusing, and survivally dangerous to terrestrial existence. They are described by such terms as hallucinations, delusions, psychotic states, dream-states—which denote nothing more than that they are alien to normal, domesticated tunnel reality. The confusion and fear generated by transcendental states of consciousness may be due to the possibility that they are designed for post-terrestrial existence.

Neurosomatic chemicals (e.g. cannabis) and neuroelectric chemicals (psychedelic indoles and alkaloids) have been used in the past by shamen and alchemists who have reported mystic, prophetic, other-worldly experiences. Some scholars have asserted that all cosmological religions are based upon visionary experiences produced by sacramental neurotransmitter substances. The opponents of psychoactive drugs correctly complain that they cause "other-worldly" experiences, irrelevant or even dangerous to mundane survival.

These neuro-chemicals have consistently been repressed by larval societies because, by suspending larval imprints, they detach humans from the conventional reality-islands and produce neurosomatic, neurophysical, and neurogenetic perspectives which are alien and disturbing. In the past, the use of neurochemicals has been restricted to intellectual elites, secret cults of mystics.

It would be logical to suppose that a society of caterpillars would be disturbed by the introduction of substances which would prematurely stimulate and activate butterfly contelligence in earth bound creatures. The orderly sequence of metamorphosis would be upset and species survival threatened if a sizable percentage of caterpillars were to rush around communicating prophetic visions of gaudy-winged existence.

Since 1945 the nervous systems and DNA of humans has been exposed to three powerful mutation-causing stimuli which are new to the species:

— radio-activity due to X-rays and nuclear explosions
— electromagnetic and electronic radiation generated by technology
— neurosomatic and neurophysical drugs, additives and synthetics in diet, chemical pollutions in the atmosphere.

Exo-psychology suggests that exposure to these powerful electrochemical energies has set in motion an expected mutational process—that DNA, in response, has signalled the nervous system of those born after 1945 that the time has come to mutate. It is time to begin migrating from the planet.

There is no reason to suppose that television, nuclear fission and fusion, neuro-somatic and neuroelectric drugs are unexpected by DNA or are unusual to this planet. The assumption is made that the creation of an oxygen atmosphere by primordial vegetation which triggered off the DNA pre-programmed construction of gills and lungs occurs as a standard evolutionary sequence on every habitable planet. The further assumption is made that electronics, nuclear fission, synthetic chemicals and neuro-active drugs are energy transformations expected by DNA and serve as triggering mechanisms to activate the next mutation. Billions of similar planets have suffered through Hiroshimas, youth-drug cults, and prime-time television. Metamorphosis is surprising to the individual to whom it is happening but not to DNA.

The egocentricity of larval philosophers inevitably leads to frustration and guilt. "Men" who think they uniquely control and dominate nature feel responsible and remorseful when events turn-out to their disadvantage. Over-population and pollution, for example, become "sins" in a new larval-survival morality.

Neurogenetics and exo-psychology on the other hand teach a modest, optimistic trust in the intelligence of DNA. The genetic code knows what SHe is doing. Neuro-active drugs appear exactly when they are needed by RNA. The multi-billion year interstallar plan of DNA is not going to be surprised or blocked by Los Angeles smog, or acid-rock, or Malthusian inflation, or radiation fall-out.

Doomsday scenarios and Spenglerian scripts are larval fears of personal mortality. Eschatological fantasies of the menopausal. We recall that "everyone" thought that the world would end in the year 1000 A.D. How presumptious of "man" to worry that "he" can do anything—good or bad—to interfere with a multi-billion year old evolutionary process which is unfolding in exactly the same way on millions of similar planets throughout the galaxy.*

---

*At this exact moment on other planets there are undoubtedly several thousand philosophers imprisoned for mutational ideas typewriting exo-psychological texts and millions of readers, like yourself, uneasily wondering if there really are millions of readers like yourself on other planets; a bit disturbed by the possibility that evolution operates the same way throughout the galaxy and that "today" has occurred millions of times before.

Every new level of energy discovered by "man"—chemical, electronic, nuclear—
is surprising, dismaying, confusing to the imprinted mind. But to DNA the appearance
of new chemicals or electro-magnetic stimuli is simply signal that a more advanced
phase of evolution is about to happen.

The widespread use of neuro-active drugs may be a sign that a new level of contelligence is emerging. Neurosomatic drugs loosen the synaptic connections which
define larval reality and dramatically extend and intensify sensory-somatic awareness.
Cannabis diminishes emotional, mental, and social commitments and produces a
detached, amused hedonism, a heightened sensitivity to raw, direct sensuality.

Cannabis is a neurosomatic trigger activating a new neural circuit. It is no accident that cannabis becomes the culture-symbol of the first generation of the mass-
technological society.

The discovery of the body, the exploration of the body, the aestheticization
of the body is the first step in freeing the nervous system from larval life-lines to
the earth—and preparation for zero-gravity.

STAGE 13: NEUROSOMATIC RECEPTIVITY

The first post-larval stage; the body free from the neuro-umbilical imprints ready for zero-gravity existence. This is the recapitulation of Stage 1, when, immediately after birth, the neonate rests without neural links to the environment.

In Stage 13 the body is temporarily detached from external imprinted connections, and becomes a zero-gravity instrument. This is called being "high." The first reaction to a new neural circuit is exploratory. Intake. Passive receptivity to the new signals. The body becomes the source of pleasure. Self-identification as a Hedonic consumer.

The attitude is floating selfishness. Why struggle for external material rewards (emotional, mental, social) which are clumsy artificial symbolic triggers for the sensory-somatic-endocrine experience? The external reward-triggers can be suspended by ingesting the neuro-chemical. After the adult has mastered the four larval survival dials, the robot addiction to the material world can be "kicked." The high body is natural. "Normal" symbolic reality is seen as larval crutch.

There are four anti-materialist neurosomatic revelations that come to the intelligent drug user—vegetative, emotional, mental and social.

1. Why rely on materialistic stimuli for the feeling of vegetative wellbeing, when a drug can trigger-off cellular satisfaction and eliminate pain?

2. Why sweat and struggle for the material-muscular rewards which give emotional satisfaction—the Cadillac, the title, the house on the hill—when a drug can activate the neural state of freedom? Einsteinian mobility replaces Newtonian pushing.

3. Why go on repeating symbol sequences or artifact-manufacturing processes, why continue stereotype robot mental routines, when a drug can free the mind to make new connections and fresh creative solutions? Why be a machine-like assembly-line reactor, when the loose, relaxed, floating mind can bend, curve and slide symbols in the rhythms and sequences of the natural? Why work when the universe is a playful energy field?

4. And why, for the brief pleasure of genital orgasm, commit oneself to a life of domesticated slavery when a neurosomatic drug can produce direct, naked sensation in which every touch, taste, smell, movement, sight, sound explodes in somatic rapture?

Neuroactive drugs have been used since the dawn of history by those who wish "to escape" to the internal pleasures of the sensory-somatic.

What is it that the cannabis user escapes from? The moralistic answer: from social responsibility. The neurological answer: escape from the tunnel-reality of the four artificial imprints.

The first post-larval stage (13) is infantile self-indulgence. Establishing a new ego-identity. The Hippie movement. The passive hedonist. Moralists complain that the youth culture is infantile. Exactly. As aimless and unproductive as a baby. The first post-larval generation (those born between 1945 and 1970) naturally bore the brunt of mutational confusion. We can imagine that the first generation of amphibians were similarly misunderstood as crazy, lazy mixed-up kids, laying around on the shoreline passively enjoying the naked sun and sniffing oxygen.

The later post-larval generations will be helped by the experiences and the compassion of those who preceded them.*

---

*Time projections, forward or back, are always intriguing. If we knew then. . .could Hiroshima have been prevented? If this book and the neurogenetic principles it presents had been available in the 1960's much confusion might have been avoided. Idle speculation. DNA expects that the first reaction to a new energy will be self-indulgent and confused.

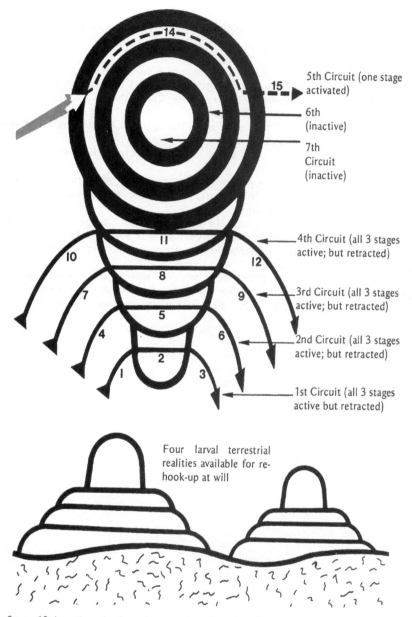

5th Circuit (one stage activated)

6th (inactive)

7th Circuit (inactive)

4th Circuit (all 3 stages active; but retracted)

3rd Circuit (all 3 stages active; but retracted)

2nd Circuit (all 3 stages active; but retracted)

1st Circuit (all 3 stages active but retracted)

Four larval terrestrial realities available for re-hook-up at will

Stage 13 is activated when the mutation from larval-terrestrial to extra-terrestrial neurology occurs. The four larval imprint fibers are retracted and the body operates as poly-sensory time-ship. Phylogenetically this stage defines the 1st post-terrestrial Stage. While every post-terrestrial passes through this stage, the human who is genetically wired to play this role is called Pisces II, the Hedonic Consumer.

STAGE 14: NEUROSOMATIC INTELLIGENCE

The receptive stage of a mutational advance is followed by an integrative stage. Just as the endomorphic Biosurvival imprint (Stage 1) is followed by viscerotonic conditioning—discriminatory and selective (Stage 2)—so does Stage 14 organize and control the neurosomatic signalry of Stage 13.

At Stage 13 the neural lines to the umbilical external are retracted. The sensory-somatic signals are received. Sensory consumerism emerges.

The body-brain then begins to select, remember, relate, control somatic-sensory function; Stage 14.

The preceding stage (13) is personified by the passive, floating Hippie; Stage 14 by the disciplined yogin, health-food adept, body-wizard, who attains precise control, learns to operate the body time-ship.

The first post-larval generation believed naively that "turning on" was an end-point. Feel-good consumerism. A small percentage were sophisticated enough to study and master the management of sensuality, to chart and navigate the infinite internal geography of neurophysiology.

The vague, theosophical cliche "look within," now takes on specific anatomical meaning. "Look within" means within the body. Control of the autonomic nervous system, of somatic reactions which are involuntary and unconscious to the larval.

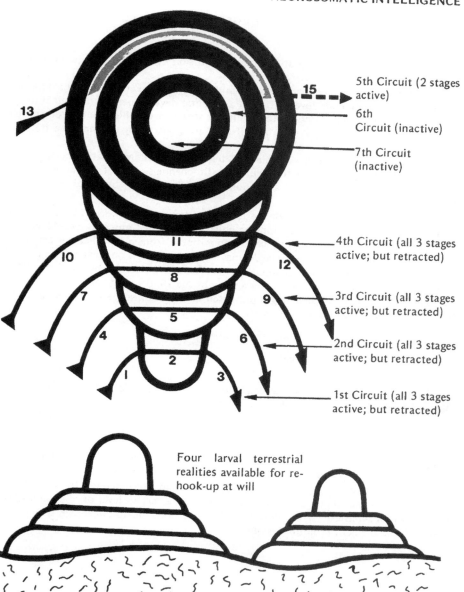

5th Circuit (2 stages active)

6th Circuit (inactive)

7th Circuit (inactive)

4th Circuit (all 3 stages active; but retracted)

3rd Circuit (all 3 stages active; but retracted)

2nd Circuit (all 3 stages active; but retracted)

1st Circuit (all 3 stages active; but retracted)

Four larval terrestrial realities available for re-hook-up at will

Stage 14 is activated when the Fifth Brain learns to control, integrate, organize, remember neurosomatic signals and manipulate the poly-sensory, gravity free body. Phylogenetically this stage represents the Fifth Brain. While every post-terrestrial passes through this stage, the human who is genetically wired to play this role is called Aries II; the Yogin, the Body Consciousness.

STAGE 15: NEUROSOMATIC FUSION

After reception and integration comes the fusion of the new energy with others to form the social linkage. Synergy.

Neural circuits are designed to transmit, communicate, hook-up. The linkage—poetically called union or love—is not an accidental development. It is built into the DNA design. Fusion and inter-change produce a structure capable of increased contelligence. Two heads are better than one—if they are transceiving on the same frequencies.

Our language does not have a scientific term for this communication between two or more persons operating on the neurosomatic channels, free of symbolic-material imprints. It has been called Extra-symbolic Perception (ESP). Spiritual community. Agape. Tantra.

The neurological awakening of the 1960's has resulted in a widespread fascination with pesonal growth and self-development which is called the Consciousness Movement. The general tendency to withdraw blind commitment from political-career activities, the skepticism and challenge to cliche dogma, the new emphasis on personal as opposed to public values has led some social critics like Thomas Wolfe to wonder if the "Me" generation is a return to the Eisenhower apathy of the 1950's.

The theory of mutational stages presented in this book suggests that there are no "returns" in nature but rather, cycles of:

> reception
> integration
> transmission-linkage

at higher levels of energy.

Stage 13 (Hedonic Consumer) leads to Stage 14 (Hedonic Self Actualizer). And Stage 14 leads in turn to Stage 15—the formation of Neurosomatic groups. The many cults, sects, consciousness movements which blossomed in the 1970's are examples of Stage 15 linkage.

The "apathy" of the post 60's generation is deceptive. Youth today is highly engaged in interna-somatic experimentation and is less than enthusiastic about committing to old-style political, social or religious doctrines. One of the most interesting (and predictable) aspects of current (1976) neurosociology is the electric acceptance of S.M.I^2.L.E. concepts by those who have attained a certain level of "Self-actualization-and-sensory-mastery" and who are waiting to hook up to collectives which will make possible the next evolutionary step.

5th Circuit (all 3 stages active)

6th Circuit (inactive)

7th Circuit (inactive)

4th Circuit (all 3 stages active; but retracted)

3rd Circuit (all 3 stages active; but retracted)

2nd Circuit (all 3 stages active; but retracted)

1st Circuit (all 3 stage active; but retracted)

Four larval terrestrial realities available for re-hook-up at will

Stage 15 is activated when the Fifth Brain hooks up with other poly-sensory time-ships and forms Neurosomatic Fusions. Phylogenetically this stage defines the first direct energy-communication between humans. While every post-larval is designed to pass through this stage, those who are genetically wired to play this role are called Taurus II; the Tantric Fusion.

STAGE 16: NEUROELECTRIC RECEPTIVITY

The Sixth Circuit emerges when the nervous system begins to understand and control its own functioning as a bio-electric transceiver.

By comparison, when the Fifth Circuit is activated, the nervous system begins to understand and control its somatic vehicle, floating unattached to fixed terrestrial locale.

When the Sixth Circuit is activated, the nervous system real-izes that it is a transceiver for bio-electric frequencies. We speak here of what has been poetically called "the sixth sense." The ability, manifested by certain premature larvals, to pick up messages beyond the audio-visual-tactile-chemical range of the neurosomatic circuit.

The telepathic facility is not unusual. A surprisingly high percentage of larvals will report in confidence that they have experienced pre-cognition or distance reception. These episodes are uncanny to the larval. Shrouded in taboo. The Catholic church has traditionally considered such "psychic" phenomena as sinful or diabolic. Respectable scientists prudishly avoid discussion or examination of the widespread evidence for the existence of "Sixth sense" data.

It is well known that lower species can transceive electromagnetic and gravitational signals. The homing and migratory skills of birds depends on their accurate reception of electro-gravitational energies. The bio-rhythms of all species seem to be activated by electro-magnetic messagery. Although it is obvious that all nervous systems operate as electro-magnetic transceivers, the implications for human psychology have been ignored.

This superstitious avoidance of a powerful human ability is genetically valid. Most human taboos and bizarre moral codes are grounded in neurologic or genetic wisdom. Just as neurosomatic (hedonic), imprint-retracting drugs are unsettling to a larval society, so are neurophysical experiences distracting and survivally confusing. The four-brained social robot is designed to limit Hir perspective to the immediate environment. The insect who leaves the pathways of the anthill to wander off, trying to communicate with humans is sensed as a danger to the hive.

Contelligent use of the neurophysical circuit had to await the development of electronic and atomic technology to provide the language and models. The nervous system has served, since the beginning of biological evolution, as a transceiver for electro-magnetic-gravitational signals, but only with the onset of atomic technology, in preparation for space migration, does the Sixth Circuit become available for conscious communication. The robots begin to learn how to operate their own circuitry.

Stage 16 is the passive, exploratory phase of the neuroelectric experience. Self-indulgent reception. It should be noted that in most cases of "psychic" phenomena, the so-called "sensitive" receives. There are fewer cases of persons becoming transmitters of neurophysical signals. This illustrates the childhood quality of the receptive phase of new circuits.

Another example of neurophysical receptivity comes from radio-astronomy. Great "dishes" scan the sky receiving electromagnetic signals. Less energy is devoted to sending messages out into space with the intent of conscious communication. This reflects the instinctive awareness that humanity is an immature species—passively waiting to be contacted. The same is true of the U.F.O. phenomenon. Opinion polls reveal that more than 50% of the American public believes in the existence of extraterrestrial visitations. Very few of these believers ever consider that they, personally, could be part of an extra-terrestrial expedition [Stage 18], which lies ahead in the human future.

Circuit 6 is activated by neuro-electric drugs. Certain organic chemicals derived from ergot, cactus, mushrooms allow the nervous system to become aware of its role as transceiver of physical energy. We must be precise about the chain of causation. The drugs do not stimulate the neuro-electric activity. The brain is a bio-electric network and has been transceiving these signals for two billion years. The drugs apparently dissolve synaptic barriers which prevent the larval mind from being aware of the molecular transactions and bio-electric signals which are the moment-to-moment commerce of the brain.

The myriad somatic and physiological events made conscious when the neuro-somatic circuit is opened up were ongoing since birth. Neurosomatic chemicals simply lower the synaptic gates which keep the Third Circuit symbolic mind from being aware of the involuntary activity.

At Stage 16 the post-larval human becomes aware of the bio-electric nature of brain activity. It is like removing the panels which protect the computer and exposing the detailed operation of the circuitry—a revelation which would be distracting to the pilot flying the computer-controlled plane. The pilot simply wants the directional read-out; and the larval does not want to know that his dinner is made up of atoms which are themselves tiny particles whirling through space. He wants solid meat on a solid plate.

The reality of interstellar existence is, however, very different. Electro-magnetic-gravitational processes are the meat and potatoes of galactic life. The vibratory-transceiver nature of the brain, useless to the larval, is very necessary in space. Telepathy. Brain-computer links. Brain-radio connections. Cyborg symbiosis.

Extra-terrestrial events are measured in terms of light-speed. Extra-terrestrial communication involves not laryngeal-manual symbols on paper or words vocalized along sound-wave frequencies, but the wide spectrum of electronic signals.

The caricature Stage 16 personage is the "acid head" wandering around with unfocused eyes, exclaiming "Wow! It's all vibrations." We recall the cliche putdown of the acid-head who looks at the desk in front of him and says "Wow! A pencil!" It is easy to ridicule such a precarious and vulnerable mutant and to sniff distainfully about LSD confusions. Actually, the unfortunate acid-head is performing a tremendous epistemological feat for which he is quite unprepared and to which his larval culture is stupidly unsympathetic. When he says "Wow! A pencil!" he is identifying a whirlpool cluster of electrons with the correct English name! He is accomplishing an Einsteinian intellectual task.

The astonishing spiritual brutality and know-nothing vulgarity of the Nixon era made it fashionable and safe to derogate and bully the users of LSD who, ill prepared and untutored, were performing a recklessly gallant genetic function. The first humans to deliberately use the brain as radio transceiver and to experience the basic electronic nature both of the brain and the universe it inhabits.

Sophisticated Stage 16 psychedelicists fell back on the pre-scientific ontology of Hinduism—"All is Maya (illusion)" or "All is Lila (play of energy)." Hinduism is a passive-receptive philosophy, basically correct in its ontology and neurogenetic cosmology, but anti-intellectual and pre-scientific.

Buddhism, a more elegant, quietist doctrine, also accepts the vibratory nature of reality, but advocates an aesthetic, here-and-now passivity and indifference. The books of Carlos Castaneda present a peyote-cult version of the neuro-electric experience:

"separate realities." Since the uneducated Yaqui Indian, don Juan, is not familiar with atomic physics, he uses the vocabulary of magic and power to describe experiences which are unmistakably neuro-electric.

Stage 16, like all receptive stages, is exploratory and childishly passive. The pop-eyed acid-head is a transient evolutionary form. Neuro-electric drugs like LSD are not designed for terrestrial life and are rightly considered dangerous by larval moralists. The Sixth Circuit is designed for extra-terrestrial life—and its activation by drugs at the present time is in preparation for migration. Neurophysical drugs can be used by neuro-logicians to "cure" ineffective childhood imprints. LSD-type drugs used for treatment or for pre-flight training should be administered by knowledgeable experts who under-stand the principles of re-imprinting and who have experiential control of their own nervous systems. The hedonic "party" use of LSD is a risky business. It is true that the ecstasy of direct vibratory reality is intense, far beyond the delights of larval rewards and material pleasures, and it is true that the ontological revelations allow one to experience elemental Einsteinian reality (of which imprints are the static, faded copies). However, physical reality is too explosive an experience for mundane expo-sure. The brain is an extra-terrestrial organ. The brain is an alien intelligence. The brain has no more concern for earthly affairs than the cultured, sympathetic traveller for the native village in which SHe spends the night.

The discovery that the brain, which one has naively considered one's own ego-tool, is actually an alien presence (viewing the host-personality with the aesthetic eye which an elegant aristocrat might cast upon an ignorant, gross, uneducated, opiniona-ted, irascible rural inn-keeper) is shocking to the unprepared LSD-user and can lead to frenzies of shame and humiliation. The so-called "bad trip" is often nothing more than the "ego" viewing itself through the clear lens of its own Higher Intelligence.

There is another LSD-myth which can be understood in the light of neuro-logic. This is the apocryphical legend that neurophysical drugs can cause people to want to jump out windows. We are aware, of course, that the defenestration myth becomes a self-fulfilling prophecy. Once given rumor-currency, the vulnerability of the imprint-retracted state can give reality to the myth. "I am now free to create a new reality. What does one do in the Nirvana state? Oh yes, I remember. Find a window to jump out of. That's what Reader's Digest suggested."

Behind the suggestive power of the legend we find the evolutionary meaning. LSD activates post-terrestrial contelligence. Humanity's home is in space. Humanity's natur-al atmosphere is zero-gravity. We are designed to float, to evolve into flight, to swim around in null-G freedom.

Stage 16 neurophysical hedonism is a natural, youthful reaction to the newly acquired experience. During its larval existence, the brain has been buffered and sealed off from electromagnetic vibratory reality. The artifacts and machines produced by the Third Circuit brutalize and coarsen experience. The heavy, slow somatic functions of the Fifth Circuit are encumbrances. Neurosomatic experience is filtered through the slow liquid transactions of cellular organs.

Sixth Circuit consciousness, however, is crystal clear, radiant, electric, frictionless, unencumbered by material inertias. It is understandable that a period of self-indulgent playing with raw, direct, smooth humming energy would occur.

At Stage 16 the neuro-electric child plays with the electro-magnetic-signals. The next step is the intelligent integration and reconstruction of the new energy forms.

5th Circuit (all 3 stages activated)

6th Circuit (one stage active)

7th Circuit (inactive)

4th Circuit (all 3 stages active; but retracted)

3rd Circuit (all 3 stages active; but retracted)

2nd Circuit (all 3 stages active; but retracted)

1st Circuit (all 3 stages active; but retracted)

Four larval terrestrial realities available for re-hook-up at will

Stage 16 is the first, exploratory slot of the Neuro-electric circuit. The Brain, freed from the body and the four terrestrial imprints, operates as a neuro-computer. Neuro-electric passivity. Einstein consciousness. Self-definition as a bio-electric computer, self-indulgent use of electronics. While every post-human is designed to pass through this Stage, the human who is genetically wired to play this role is called GEMINI II.

STAGE 17: NEURO-ELECTRIC INTELLIGENCE

The passivity of the receptive stage, waiting to receive what gets "dished up," becomes confusing and frustrating. Eventually one begins to wonder about the mechanisms and lawful meanings of the phenomena. The neuro-electric intelligence becomes selective, experimental, recollective. One learns from the passive experiences, learns how to control and direct the energies involved.

This book, and this section of the book in particular, is a crude symbolization of neuro-electric events. A manual on how to use the electronic transceiver we call the brain.

Our current ability to "think" about neurophysical energies (i.e. to connect L.M. symbols with atomic events) is due to two recent scientific advances: the theoretical models and formulae of atomic physicists and the experiential reports of those whose Sixth Circuits have been activated by neurotransmitter drugs.

We have noted that each new evolving circuit of the nervous system includes and inter-connects with those that precede it. The Sixth Circuit is the central bio-computer. It receives signals from the other five circuits (and, as we shall see, from RNA-DNA). These signals, regardless of their original sensory location, reach the brain as electro-chemical "bleeps." The Sixth Circuit brain also receives signals from molecular memory banks within neurons—also in the form of "off-on" bleeps.

During larval existence, the Sixth Circuit is mainly concerned with mediating the terrestrial survival-traffic from the four-umbilical circuits.

When the Sixth Brain is activated, a long, complex and disciplined training is required to establish conscious integrated control.

Humanity is just now beginning to understand that the brain is a transceiving-computing instrument which can be used to communicate at electronic speeds and frequencies. The Sixth Brain cannot be used to operate in larval environments, cannot slow down to the Newtonian rate of emotion-muscular, manual-mental, or domestic-social exchanges of "island-realities."

The Sixth Circuit capacity of the brain operates best in a protective environment which responds at Einsteinian speeds and relativities—or at least where the others present refrain from imposing larval signals on the transception.

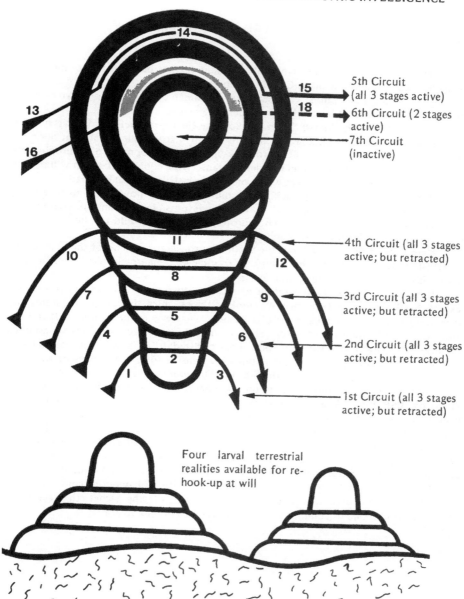

5th Circuit (all 3 stages active)

6th Circuit (2 stages active)

7th Circuit (inactive)

4th Circuit (all 3 stages active; but retracted)

3rd Circuit (all 3 stages active; but retracted)

2nd Circuit (all 3 stages active; but retracted)

1st Circuit (all 3 stages active; but retracted)

Four larval terrestrial realities available for re-hook-up at will

Stage 17 is activated when the Sixth Brain learns to control, integrate, organize Neuro-electric signals and manipulate the neuro-electricity of the brain—unencumbered by the limitations of somatic or larval-survival imprints. While every post-terrestrial human passes through this stage, the human who is genetically wired to play this role is called CANCER II.

STAGE 18: NEURO-ELECTRIC FUSION

Neuro-electric Fusion: the synergistic communication between two or more contelligences operating at the Sixth Circuit. Telepathy.

The highest, fastest, most complex form of human communication—two or more nervous systems transceiving at electro-magnetic velocities.

The abilities of the human brain to exchange electro-magnetic signals has not yet been explored. It is possible that the brain is designed to decode signals that our electronic machines are too insensitive to pick-up. The development of neurophysical contelligence may make it possible to design transceiving equipment which will permit the reception of complex messages which only a bio-instrument can originate.

Humans have constructed machines to amplify muscular power. In similar fashion, cyborg neuro-electronic equipment may make it possible to transmit contelligent messages across great distances. Such neurophysical signals would not be in terms of L.M. symbols, but direct neural-energy units.

Here it must be re-stated that the Sixth (Neuro-electric) circuit of the brain is not a terrestrial survival organ. The ability to transceive at neuro-electric intensities and speeds is designed for post-terrestrial existence.

It is true that in every generation of recorded history certain premature evolutes exhibit Sixth Circuit contelligence. We think of the psychics, the fey, the mediums, the revelatory prophets, the great mystic philosophers—as well as the idiot savants and the strange eccentric geniuses who for centuries have been carted off to insane asylums because they saw too much too soon. Less civilized tribes have often instinctively understood that strange mental perceptions are signs of futique endowment and have defined socially accepted roles for the Sixth Circuit prematures.

While there is no doubt that extraordinary neural abilities occur in some humans—telepathy, ESP, psychokinesis, strange mathematical and symbolic accomplishments—it is also true that such people find no place in larval society. It is possible that ESP, for example, is a post-terrestrial trait. Those who have been endowed with this ability may be in the position of fish with vocal cords or mammals with symbolic abilities. To attempt telepathy down here on the bottom of a four-thousand mile atmospheric swamp would be like attempting oral conversation under water. The blurps and bubbles would conceal the fact that once out of water a new form of symbolic conversation is available. It is probable that once we have migrated off the planet, the telepathic (neuro-electric) mode of communication will become common-place.

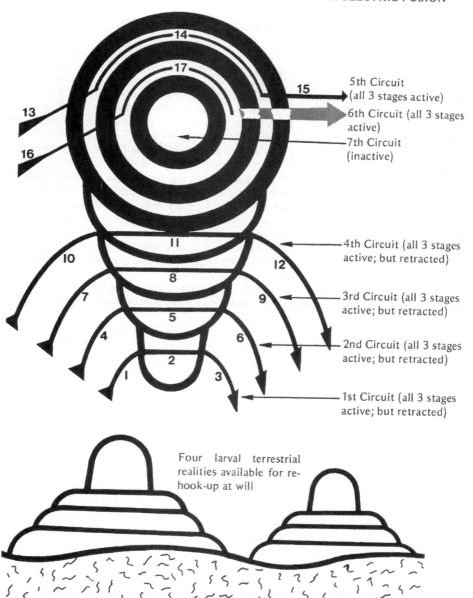

5th Circuit
(all 3 stages active)

6th Circuit (all 3 stages active)

7th Circuit (inactive)

4th Circuit (all 3 stages active; but retracted)

3rd Circuit (all 3 stages active; but retracted)

2nd Circuit (all 3 stages active; but retracted)

1st Circuit (all 3 stages active; but retracted)

Four larval terrestrial realities available for re-hook-up at will

Stage 18 is activated when the Sixth Brain hooks up with other Sixth Brain entities and communicates at neuro-electric velocities. While every post-terrestrial passes through this Stage, the human who is genetically wired to play this role is called LEO II.

Telepathic Linkage.

STAGE 19: NEUROGENETIC RECEPTIVITY

The Seventh Circuit. The nervous system receiving signals from DNA.

DNA designs and constructs nervous systems and maintains supervisory and re-constructive communication with somatic cells and neurons mediated by RNA.

The nervous system continually receives DNA and RNA signals. Inside the nucleus of every neuron, there "lives" a DNA master-plan which contains a record of the chain of bodily re-incarnations back to the origin of life on this planet.

Geneticists are now learning how to decipher the conversation between DNA and the body and between DNA and the nervous system.

When the Seventh Circuit of the nervous system is activated, the signals from DNA become conscious. This experience is chaotic and confusing to the unprepared person—thousands of genetic memories flash by, the molecular family-picture-album of species consciousness and evolution. This experience provides glimpses and samples of the broad design of the multi-billion year old genetic panorama.

Neurogenetic consciousness is not restricted to past perspectives. The outlines of the future DNA blueprint are also available—Psi Phy visions and pre-views—exalting and frightening—of the per-mutations which are to come.

We have seen that the first stage of any new level of con-telligence is receptive and passive-spectator. Neural entertainment and exploration is thus the function of muta-tional Stage 19.

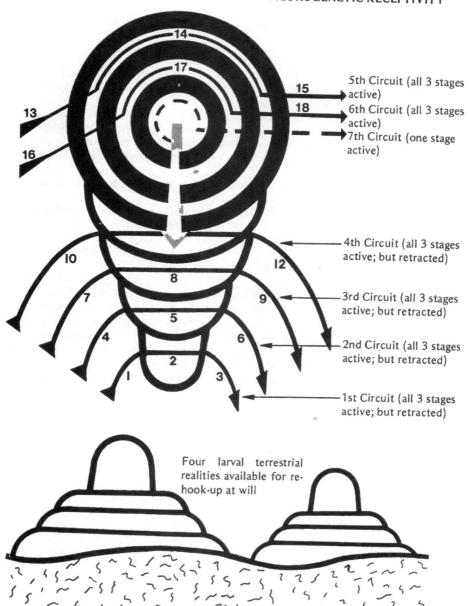

5th Circuit (all 3 stages active)

6th Circuit (all 3 stages active)

7th Circuit (one stage active)

4th Circuit (all 3 stages active; but retracted)

3rd Circuit (all 3 stages active; but retracted)

2nd Circuit (all 3 stages active; but retracted)

1st Circuit (all 3 stages active; but retracted)

Four larval terrestrial realities available for re-hook-up at will

Stage 19 is activated when the mutation is made to Neuro-genetic signals. The nervous system imprints the DNA code and tranceives RNA-DNA signals at the molecular level. While every post-human is designed to pass through this stage, those who are genetically wired to play this role are called VIRGO II.

/ 121

STAGE 20: NEUROGENETIC INTELLIGENCE

Selection, discrimination, organization, evaluation of genetic signals.

The neurogenetic circuit begins to think like DNA, learns the vocabulary of RNA. Begins to identify with the genetic intelligence which deals in the span of species and encompasses the bulti-billion year network of life.

There is no language for larval intelligence to describe the complexity and variety of the DNA design, but we can predict the emergence of genetic wizards, DNA engineers who understand the alphabet of DNA and can decipher, write, and re-write in amino-acid script, the book written in the vocabulary of guanine, adenine, cytosine, and thymine.

The function of Neurogenetic Intelligence is, of course, to stop the programmed aging process.

The basic goal of Life is Immortality. Increased Intelligence (neural control) and Space Migration are simply tools to assist in the Life Extension process.

Immortality is attained through control of the DNA—Stage 20.

To control the genetic code it is necessary to receive DNA-RNA signals and to experientially resonate, identify with them (Stage 19).

Alan Harrington has presented the external side of the Neurogenetic Wizard: ". . . salvation belongs to medical engineering and nothing else; . . . man's fate depends first on the proper management of his technical proficiency; . . . our Messiahs will be wearing white coats, not in asylums, but in chemical and biological laboratories."*

What Harrington's brilliant analysis fails to point out is that the genetic engineers of Stage 20 will use as their basic instrument their own brains, open to and conscious of neurogenetic signals. Only the DNA neuron link-up can produce the immortality and symbiotic linkage with other species—which are themselves different letters in the genetic alphabet.

---

* Harrington, Alan, *The Immortalist*, Random House, 1969.

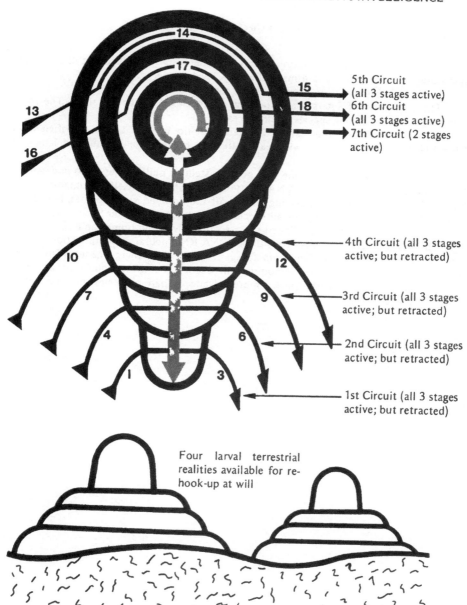

14

17

13

16

15 5th Circuit (all 3 stages active)

18 6th Circuit (all 3 stages active)

7th Circuit (2 stages active)

4th Circuit (all 3 stages active; but retracted)

10

12

3rd Circuit (all 3 stages active; but retracted)

7

9

2nd Circuit (all 3 stages active; but retracted)

4

6

1st Circuit (all 3 stages active; but retracted)

1

3

Four larval terrestrial realities available for re-hook-up at will

Stage 20 is activated when the Seventh Brain learns to control, integrate, organize Neuro-genetic signals and manipulate Chromosome. While every post-terrestrial human is designed to pass through this stage, those genetically wired to play this role are called LIBRA II.

STAGE 21: NEUROGENETIC FUSION

Neurogenetic fusion: communication with other genetic intelligences. Interspecies symbiosis. The link-up of organisms at the DNA level of energy.

Interspecies pro-creation—conscious and planful.

The formation of interstellar groupings of species. Seed cooperation. The fertilizing conversation among species intelligences.

It is obvious that when Stage 20 Neurogenetic Wizards become proficient in DNA-RNA conversation they will realize that all organic life is a unified language system.

Alan Harrington is one of the first post-Einsteinian philosophers who understood the purpose of life—"man. . . is DNA's way of understanding itself." Humanity plays a critical but transient role in getting all life off the doomed womb-planet. Humanity is the DNA engineer—working for all species—past and future. After Space Migration— an Immortal, Neurologically proficient species will evolve from homo sapiens.

The key to higher intelligence is direct DNA-RNA-neural communication among species. When the Genetic Engineers (Stage 20) begin to merge genes with other species—conscious interspecies symbiosis will occur. The most significant of these genetic fusions will be with species more advanced than ourselves—i.e. our selves in the future.

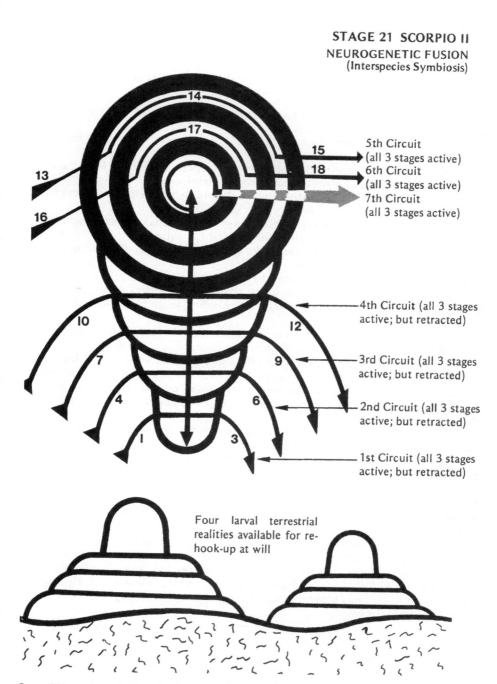

14

17

13

16

15 5th Circuit
(all 3 stages active)

18 6th Circuit
(all 3 stages active)

7th Circuit
(all 3 stages active)

10

12

7

9

4

6

1

3

4th Circuit (all 3 stages active; but retracted)

3rd Circuit (all 3 stages active; but retracted)

2nd Circuit (all 3 stages active; but retracted)

1st Circuit (all 3 stages active; but retracted)

Four larval terrestrial realities available for re-hook-up at will

Stage 21 is activated when the Seventh Brain hooks up with other Neurogenetic Entities. Interspecies Symbiosis. Communication between Neurogenetic entities by means of amino acid signalry. While every post-terrestrial is designed to pass through this stage, those genetically wired to play this role are called SCORPIO II.

STAGE 22: METAPHYSIOLOGICAL RECEPTIVITY

The reader is by now aware that exo-psychology assumes a hierarchy of contelligence which operates on a galactic scale.

After retracting earth-imprints, human contelligence centers in the body (Circuit 5).

The Sixth Period of evolution begins when intelligence retracts from the body and imprints the nervous system as electromagnetic transceiver.

The Seventh Period of evolution begins when contelligence centers in the RNA-DNA structure.

The Eighth Period of evolution begins when neurogenetic consciousness contacts and is imprinted by sub-atomic quantum-mechanical contelligence.

The paradox is consistent. The wider the scope of energy—in time/space, the more miniaturized the brain-center.

The body is controlled and directed by the brain.

The brain is designed/constructed and controlled by genetic intelligence which contains, within the nucleus of the cell, the blueprint design for billions of years of evolution.

The logical extrapolation of this process is to locate the master-plan which designs and constructs molecules, including DNA, within the nucleus of the atom.

Locating a higher intelligence within the atomic nucleus is teleological and speculative. It is a simple and heuristic answer to the ultimate challenging question which, although avoided by everyone else, cannot be avoided by the philosopher. It is the occupational hazard of the philosophic profession to be confronted by the persistent demand:

"Very well, you say that genetic intelligence is the immortal, invisible soul that outlives the body. But where does DNA come from?" or,

"Very well, you say that life was seeded on this planet by advanced forms of genetic intelligence. Who created DNA?"

On the basis of the scientific evidence now at hand, the best answer to the Higher Intelligence Creator question comes from the frontiers of nuclear physics and quantum mechanics. The basic energies, the meta-physiological contelligence is probably located within the nucleus of the atom.

In the exo-psychological manuals, **The Periodic Table of Energy** and The Game of Life, it is suggested that the Periodic Table of Elements is a basic code which transmits the evolutionary design. Each chemical element is seen as a letter in a basic energy alphabet with which nuclear contelligence writes the script of the universe. Molecules—including DNA, are texts communicated by Higher Intelligence. Super-neurons in the universal nervous system.

Such speculations are "far out" but they are surely no less believable than the orthodox Christian, Moslem, Hebraic, Hindu, Buddhist cosmologies. And they are certainly more credible than the blind-chance statistical theories of materialist scientists. Before automatically rejecting neuro-nuclear theories the reader is requested to suggest a more logical and heuristic cosmology.*

---

*The theologically sophisticated reader will note that exo-psychology presents in scientific language and in a heuristic context, classic Catholic doctrine. The soul (DNA) rises to heaven (planetary migration) and joins the community of Saints (precedent DNA contelligence) to converse and unify with the Creator.

To locate Higher Intelligence in atomic nuclei which link up and communicate across inter-stellar space/time dimensions is an eminently practical and empirical decision, conservatively in accord with the miniaturization trend which finds higher biological intelligence in such tiny spaces as the cellular nucleus.

The neurogenetic theory suggests that after migration from the planet post-larval humanity will learn to receive (19), integrate (20) and transmit (21) DNA-RNA signals—thus communicating with and symbiotically linking with genetic brains far more advanced in evolution. From these older and wiser brains humanity will perhaps learn how to decipher the sub-nuclear alphabet, to receive and experience the signals transmitted by sub-nuclear particles.

The stages of neuro-atomic contelligence (22, 23, 24) are presented here in per-sonalized form to encourage research and thinking about the future periods of human evolution. Physicists are currently studying the sub-nuclear realm to identify the high-velocity particles which make up the language of energy. The instrument used by these scientists is the human nervous system, expanded and sensitized by experi-mental hardware (linear accelerators, etc.). Exo-psychology seeks to provide the concepts which will allow nuclear physicists to personalize sub-nuclear events so that they can be experienced.

The great penetrations in our understanding of natural events come when the scientist succeeds in experientially empathizing with natural processes. We think of Kekule's serpent dream which set the stage for organic chemistry. And the use of the billiard-ball model by physicists to experience atomic events.

One of the most dramatic illustrations of the revelations which can accompany the direct experience of basic energy processes comes from the life of Albert Einstein, who apparently did not bother to express himself in 3rd Circuit symbols, i.e. did not talk, until the age of seven.

Legend has it, however, that this frail, Jewish lad living in exile in Switzerland, spent much of his time imagining what it would be like to be a photon.

Einstein's ability to write the basic equations of energy-matter may have resulted from his having experienced in his own body and brain the implications of light-speed travel—which had been reported for centuries by mystics and yogis who were not able to symbolize them in mathematical form.

Each cell in our body is composed of atoms. Sub-nuclear events inside each atom determine the elemental processes. Thus we can say that our bodies and our ner-vous systems are based on sub-nuclear events.

The Eighth Period of evolution involves the transception by the neurogenetic intelligence of nuclear signals. The conversation clearly exists. When post-human contelligence begins to receive sub-nuclear messages, Stage 22 will have been attained. We expect that humanity will be instructed in the reception of nuclear signals by high-er intelligences contacted after leaving the planet.

We can expect that the receptive stage (22) of neuro-atomic consciousness will, as was true with the other receptive stages (13, 16, 19), involve hedonic exploration. An immediate corollary is the practical suggestion that nuclear physicists approach the phenomena they study, not as manipulative scientists bombarding protons with the hope of winning a Nobel Prize, but as adolescents about to experience the power and thrilling revelation of a new energy level. Such a modestly personal posture will prepare them for the more complex modes of understanding (Stage 23) and fusion (Stage 24).

7th Circuit
capable of
receiving nuclear-
energy signals

6th Circuit
having imprinted
nuclear-particle
energy

5th Circuit
capable of being re-activated
but non-existant at 8th level
of Energy

Stage 22 is activated when the Neurogenetic Brain begins to receive Atomic nuclear signals. Phylogenetically this stage is meta-physiological and is personalized as Sagittarius II.

STAGE 23: NEURO-ATOMIC CONTELLIGENCE

The preceding stage exposes the brain to the high-energy language of the atomic nucleus.

Metaphysiological contelligence integrates, engineers, organizes nuclear particles. Creates atoms.

At this stage the basic energies which comprise all structure in the universe are available for management. The metaphysiological contelligence constructs atoms, DNA chains, molecules, neurons; sculpts, designs, architects all forms of matter by manipulating nuclear particles and gravitational force fields.

At this point in evolution, contelligence no longer needs bodies, neurons, DNA designs. It may be that the universe is a nervous system—a contelligent network—in which sub-nuclear structures act as basic neural signals. The space/time coordinates of the unified force-field is probably of a very different order from that of the bio-neural system—billionths-of-a-second time spans simultaneous with billions of light years.

Nuclear physicists are just now developing a vocabulary for Sub-Atomic Nuclear Events (S.A.N.E.). Ascertaining the semantic meaning of units of contelligence such as muons, lepton, bosons, hadrons, J-Psi particles is the beginning step in the understanding of the metaphysiological "brain."

These speculations may seem fanciful and may elicit disdainful reactions from "hard-headed" scientists—but a good case can be made for their practicality. The thinking of every nuclear physicist is influenced by cosmological and teleological concepts, however vague and unconscious they may be. Every scientist was taught a philosophic system in childhood and these early religious notions have profound effects on later views of nature, even though they are usually implicit. Indeed, unconscious childhood religious assumptions are probably the basic directive and limiting factors in the way nuclear physicists deal with their data. Suppose that the scientists who now compose the membership of the American Physical Society had been, as children, regularly exposed to the Interstellar Neurogenetic theory in Sunday schools thirty years ago. If this had been the case, the first colonizing starships would have already left the solar system and our understanding of metaphysiological signals would be far more advanced.

Failure to anticipate future evolutionary possibilities is genetic stupidity. Any projections of mutations to come—as long as they are based on current scientific data—are better than none. We can only find the future if we look for it.

Equally important is the necessity to animate, personalize scientific data. All that we know about the laws of nature, about atomic and sub-atomic events, is mediated by the nervous system. All science is neuro-ecology. All our observations of the universe are neurological events. The brain is the recording instrument. Instead of forcing nature to fit the three dimenional model of our L.M. symbolic mind, we must allow our nervous systems to be imprinted by the raw data—learn to think-experience like DNA, like electrons, like sub-atomic particles.

"All of the physics of the microworld today is quantum physics. There is no competing theory. Quantum mechanics envisions the world as being made up of sudden discrete events which it describes in an essentially statistical manner... Quantum mechanics, being a theory of collectivities, doesn't say anything about the occurrence of discrete events which combine to make up its averages... It isn't quite true that quantum mechanics is silent about the occurrence of these fundamental events. It says that they are unpredictable... There events are truly lawless—quantum banditos— and it was this anarchistic aspect of the quantum picture that provoked Einstein to say that he could not believe that God played dice with the universe.

Is there a super theory that can explain these quantum events and get quantum physicists out of their government-sponsored casinos and back to the business of "real" mechanics again? Such theories are called "hidden-variable theories"...The discovery of radical anarchy at the quantum level was profoundly distressing to Victorian physicists who had set their hopes on a more predictable clockwork universe. However, some of the more intellectually flexible savants among them wondered if this deep-rooted uncertainty could be turned to some advantage. Could newly discovered freedom at the subatomic level be identified with subjectively experienced freedom of will which each of us carries inside? This pat solution to the mind/body problem has been almost unanimously rejected by the physics community for a variety of reasons. Even if some small critical system in the brain were unaccountably found to be subject to quantum fluctuations, these fluctuations would be merely random.

"Randomness is antithetical to the inner freedom which we seem to experience. Randomness is the opposite of freedom. So, in brief, run the arguments against a hidden variable theory of consciousness... It was in this climate of opinion that E. H. Walker decided to... explore in some detail possible models for the ENTRY of mind into the world of matter thru the opening provided by fundamental subquantum disorder... As his central postulate Walker asserts that any system dominated by quantum mechanical fluctuations is conscious... Human beings are an example of a particularly direct form of coupling of quantum-fluatuate Being to matter... Walker's theory envisions two worlds—the physical world of P's, (i.e. material variables such as energy, length, space and time) and the conscious hidden-variable world of C's. Together the P's and C's constitute the entire universe of being. Inert matter is made up of P's and we, when conscious are full of C-LIFE—life of the spirit. ...In certain net-like regions of the central nervous system only a few packets of transmitter substance are released for each pulse of presynaptic depolarization. It is in these loosely coupled regions of the brain that spirit takes on the human form.

"Through our still-viable connections with the world of hidden-variables (C-LIFE) we can participate in processes which appear to violate ordinary physical law. Some of our joint participations surface in the world of P's as para-psychological phenomena... What sort of entities besides ourselves occupy the subquantum worlds of C-LIFE? Is it the fabled Summerland world of departed spirits? An invisible theophany of purposive God-like beings with courts of demons and angels? Are there complex alien cultures completely independent of the physical world of P's luxuriating just beneath the surface of the phenomenal world?

"A novel first approach to an "exobiology" of subquantum alien life-styles is to not treat so-called physical phenomena as merely physical but to regard it as having "meaning" in much the same way that secret and occult meanings are found in Biblical texts by analogical and cabalistic reasoning. We construe the physical world as a vast and ongoing "message" and try to put ourselves in a position to be sensitive to what is being voiced. In this view our entire physical science of quantum mechanical averages represents only the "speech statistics" of matter's complex and lively symposium. It is the individual events themselves—the particular sequences—that contain participation in the song that is everywhere rising around us.

"Some idea of the essential strangeness which underlies the quantum level is provided by the recent theorem due to J. S. Bell's theorem which says, essentially, that if quantum mechanics gives correct results, the subquantum world must be "non-local"—connected together in an intimate way in an instantaneous web of relationships. In this view, once two particles have interacted, they are in some sense connected forever on the subquantum level. . . Once we have interacted with something or someone, are we forever connected to them? What does Bell's theorem have to say about psychometry, about the interpenetration and "stickiness" of personalities? Should we guard our hair and nail clippings against magical misuse by enemy sorcerers? How can we experimentally foster these strange linkages; what is the relative effectiveness of palmistry, massage, sexual union in increasing Bell-type interconnectedness. How about sitting together in a hot tub?. . . It may be that for reasons similar to those advanced against a hidden-variable theory of consciousness that Bell's astonishing theorem does not play any part at all in human affairs. . . The unflinching contemplation of what Bell's theorem really has to tell us about separateness may act as a kind of spiritual exercise to bring about a similar delocalized state in the mind/world of individual scientists. For those who come to understand it, Bell's theorem can act as a powerful image reminding us of Nature's ability to casually surpass our naive notions of what must be so."

Nick Herbert

5th, 6th, and 7th
Circuits, non-active
but available

Stage 23 is activated when the Eighth Brain begins to integrate and manipulate atomic-nuclear signals. Phylogenetically this stage is meta-physiological and personified as Capricorn II.

STAGE 24: METAPHYSIOLOGICAL FUSION

As we have seen in the seven preceding circuits—exploratory receptivity is followed by integrative control and then by synergistic fusion with other elements at the same level of contelligence.

Neuro-atomic fusion (star-light) involves force-fields of interstellar magnitude and implies a unified galactic consciousness.

The assumption is made that gravitational, electro-magnetic and sub-atomic force-fields that comprise the universe are part of a coherent and conscious network.

Any eschatological discussion of galactic fusion must include the phenomenon of Black Holes. Whirlpools of anti-matter.

Many astronomers believe that there are millions of Black Holes in our galaxy—indeed, that the center of our galaxy may be a Black Hole.

The intense gravitational attraction of Black Holes sucks in the surrounding matter. Black Holes, it is thought, may be the anti-matter, anti-energy counterparts of the positive universe.

Interestingly enough, many physicists are now coming to the conclusion that the elementary particles within the nucleus are Black Holes—that the "strong force" which holds the atomic nucleus together is super-gravitational.

If this theory is true, Black Holes provide the final fusions. The final vortex. The linkage of the universe of everything with the void of everything.

5th, 6th, and 7th
Circuits capable of
being reactivated by
8th Circuit intelligence.

Stage 24 is activated when the Eighth Brain links up with other Neuro-atomic Intelligences. Phylogenetically this stage of Neuro-atomic Domestication-Black Hole Fusion (?) is called Aquarius II.

ImTheStory.com

Lightning Source UK Ltd.
Milton Keynes UK
UKHW02f1249260218
318483UK00012B/929/P

9 781314 879124